Lost Souls: F

Inspiring Stories About Herding Breed Dogs

Kyla Duffy and Lowrey Mumford

Published by Happy Tails Books™, LLC

Happy Tails Books™ uses the power of storytelling to effect positive change in the lives of animals in need. The joy, hope, and (occasional) chaos these stories describe will make you laugh and cry as you em*bark* on a journey with these authors, who are guardians and/or fosters of rescued animals. "Reading for Rescue" with Happy Tails Books not only brings further awareness to animal advocacy efforts and breed characteristics, but each sale also results in a financial contribution to rescue efforts.

Lost Souls: Found!™ Inspiring Stories About Herding-Breed Dogs by Kyla Duffy and Lowrey Mumford

Published by Happy Tails Books™, LLC www.happytailsbooks.com

The publisher gratefully acknowledges the numerous rescue groups and their members, who generously granted permission to use their stories and photos.

Any brand names mentioned in this book are registered trademarks and the property of their owners. The author and publishing company make no claims to them.

Photo Credits:

> Front: *Sadie,* Emilee Fuss, http://emileefuss.com
> Back Top: *Sophie,* Mark Nardecchia, http://shagly.com
> Left: *Spirit,* Susan Papa
> Middle: *JeanLuc,* Mark Nardecchia, http://shagly.com
> Right: *Owen, Debbie Bauer,* http://www.your-inner-dog.com
> Interior Title Page: Jennifer Hague, http://fixyourimages.com
> Interior Introduction Page: *Beaux,* Mark Nardecchia, http://shagly.com

Publishers Cataloging In Publication Data Available Upon Request

ISBN: 978-0-9846801-5-3

Happy Tails Books appreciates all of the contributors and rescue groups whose thought-provoking stories make this book come to life.

A Forever Home Rescue Foundation
http://www.aforeverhome.org/

Atlantic Region Central Border Collie Rescue
http://www.arcbcr.org/

Blue Ridge Border Collie Rescue
http://www.brbcr.org/

Carolina ACD Rescue and Rebound
http://www.carolinasrescue.com/

Central Ohio Sheltie Rescue
http://centralohiosheltierescue.org/

Houston Collie Rescue
http://www.houstoncollierescue.org/

Nebraska Border Collie Rescue
http://www.nebraskabordercollierescue.com/

New Hope Cattle Dogs Rescue and Rehoming
http://www.newhopecattledogs.com/

Northern Chesapeake Sheltie Rescue
http://www.ncsr-md.org/

North Texas Corgi Rescue
http://www.petfinder.com/shelters/TX432.html/

Visit the following link for more information about the dogs, authors, and rescues featured in this book:

http://www.happytailsbooks.com/about/authors/

Table of Contents

INTRODUCTION: Too Much Trouble

Over the years we've helped find homes for many rescue dogs. These are not the dogs who do search-and-rescue, although many are capable; they are, instead, dogs in need of rescue themselves.

Rescue dogs may be surrendered by humans for reasons of health (the human's or the dog's), incompatibility, or changes in living conditions. Some come from puppy mills, large-scale breeding facilities that provide puppies from sick, poorly-treated breeding dogs to unsuspecting customers through pet shops and online. Herding-breed dogs, specifically, are often surrendered to shelters and rescues as being "too much trouble" because their owners did not understand their requirements for physical and mental stimulation beyond that of other breeds. This list is not exhaustive, but the fact remains that regardless of the reason a dog ends up in rescue, he or she needs a helping human hand.

One of our Collies, Candy, is a rescue dog twice over. She came to us last year, initially because my wife's mother had been unable to care for her dogs for a time for health reasons, but she stayed because we fell in love. She is getting old and needs some special attention, which we (humans and dogs) are more than happy to provide.

Heather's mother had first rescued Candy in San Diego more than 10 years ago, so we don't know how old she actually is. Back then Heather and I made a habit of visiting the shelters and dog pounds in the area to see whether there were Collies or Belgian Sheepdogs needing help. Of course, we felt for all the dogs there, but we could only save so many. When we found other purebred dogs awaiting their fates, we let folks from their respective rescue groups know about them, and they did the same for us. The network performs quite well.

We found Candy in a pound, not a shelter. Pounds tend to house strays *very* temporarily. If owners don't come looking for their lost dogs quickly, the dogs are usually put to sleep. Nobody was going to come for Candy. Her former owners actually put her there, probably because the local humane society asked for donations when taking in dogs. All we know about Candy is what they wrote on her kennel card before leaving: "Candy: Too much trouble." Sound familiar?

In those days the pound charged us about $100 to spring a dog. However, they only charged senior citizens $35, so to save money, we had Heather's mother get dogs out for us. In Candy's case, she was lucky that Heather's mother came quickly because she walked out the front door with only a half-hour left before her scheduled euthanasia.

Heather's mother took Candy home with her, and by the time we went to pick her up the next day, Candy had worked her magic. Heather's mother was hooked, so Candy would be staying with her.

Now, a decade later, Candy has come back to us, the humans who first saw her in that dog-pound cage, to be rescued once more. And at who-knows-how-many-years-old, she has worked her magic again, in some ways making us rescuers feel like the rescued.

I sometimes wonder what Candy was like as a baby. For all the time we've known her, she has been kind, calm, and well-behaved. I think she must have been a perfectly wonderful puppy, until I see her watching our pet bunnies through the fence. As she whirls and barks with joy, I wonder about that "too much trouble" kennel card. Maybe her first owner was a rabbit rancher?

As for us, we're glad to have our "too much trouble" dog; she turned out to be no trouble at all.

As you read through these wonderful stories about herding-breed dogs, I hope you'll consider what "too much trouble" might mean to you. I believe that adopting dogs and giving them second chances will be no trouble at all for you, either (or, at least, no more trouble than they are worth, as most adopters feel their rescued dogs have been worth their weight in gold). I can assure you, it will certainly mean the world to them. And, you never know, it might even create some magic for you, too.

 *Daniel Castle*

Inspiring Stories About
Herding-Breed Dogs

Two Tomboys Together

© K H Photography

All my life, I wanted a dog, but my parents simply were not "dog people." (I did have a pony growing up, so life wasn't all that terrible.) During undergrad, I knew I just was not capable of the responsibility, but that did not stop me from spending hours looking at Petfinder. com and crying over all the lost souls needing homes. As soon as I graduated and moved to Denver, I was ready for a dog. Two days after the move, my best friend and I spent the day looking at shelters in the city before driving 40 minutes away to a more rural shelter. We saw plenty of nice dogs, but none seemed like the right fit.

That changed as soon as Lainey was brought into an adoption room to meet us. Her sweet disposition and tail-less "bunny butt" had us from the beginning, and as soon as I said her new name – Clementine – her big Cattle Dog ears perked up, and she gave me a quick lick on the hand. I knew I had found my dog.

While the adoption counselors drew up the contract, I couldn't keep my eyes off Clementine. The staff had tied a big bow on her collar to draw attention to her since she was just about out of time. She had been at the shelter for more than two months, and no one had inquired about her. She stared back at me with her beautiful eyes, tilted her head, and then whipped it around to chew on that silly bow. Being quite the tomboy myself, I couldn't help but laugh and fall even more in love. I vowed right at that moment that the only accessory she would sport from then on would be the occasional bandana or jacket if it was really cold.

The first few months with Clem were impossibly difficult. The shelter had no history on her, just that she was another overnight drop-off, suspected to be around two years old. She was skittish and shy of everything. She constantly chewed and got in the trash. Every noise and movement caused her to roll over and pee in submission. I knew I was in trouble when I thought I could outsmart her by getting a trash can with a lid, and within five minutes of bringing it home, I caught her with one paw on the step and her head in the trash.

When I contacted the shelter's behavior helpline, they were quick to suggest giving her a job to do, attending classes that used positive training techniques, and providing lots of exercise. I started working on teaching her tricks and playing disc with her every day. Immediately, her behavior improved!

At the time, we lived in a small, one-bedroom apartment on a busy road. Every time I took Clem outside to go to the bathroom I changed from pajamas to jeans (you never know who you're going to see!). One day Clem was whining to go out, and I told her, "Hang on! You know I have to change my pants."

She cocked her head to one side and trotted off to the bedroom. Thirty seconds later she came back dragging a pair of my jeans that she had dug out of the laundry basket! I had never taught her this "trick." That's when I realized she was much smarter than I had thought.

I then started researching other activities I could do with Clem and learned about the dog sport of flyball, in which dogs work as a team to win a relay race of jumping hurdles, grabbing a ball out of a spring-loaded box, and returning it to their handlers. We were lucky to get involved with a club that really promoted rescue dogs and positive training.

Initially, classes were tough for us, and we even failed both of the beginner classes because Clem was too scared to leave me to get the ball. We kept working at it, and now she is one of the club's faster and more consistent dogs! We have been competing for more than five years now and have met some truly wonderful people because of the sport. We also compete in agility and disc and even do some herding on the side.

I have a disability that makes it difficult to move, and I have hearing loss. I have been able to train Clementine to assist me with balancing, picking up dropped objects, and alerting me to sounds I cannot hear. This little, terrified, 30-

pound shelter drop-off is now an ONYX Flyball Champion, agility title holder (many times over), service dog, and AKC Canine Good Citizen. I always wonder what those first two years were like for my peanut, but, boy, am I glad that we found each other. I simply cannot imagine life without her.

Through it all, Clementine has proved to be an amazing dog. She has opened a lot of doors in my life (literally and figuratively). Though she is getting older, she has no intention of slowing down any time soon. Her rescued Border Collie "brother" makes sure of that. She has taught me that patience and perseverance really can conquer all.

 Aly Jabrocki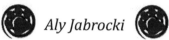

My two-year-old Sheltie (Shetland Sheepdog) needed a companion, but my 10-year-old wasn't interested in playing. In order to find a canine companion who could appease both dogs, I found myself looking into adopting an adult instead of purchasing a puppy from a reputable breeder. It was my first time considering a rescued dog.

I found Gavin on Petfinder.com. He came from a dog hoarder who had kept him outside with 72 other dogs and only a barn for shelter. I adopted him on a cold February day with no inkling of the challenge he would be.

Gavin is a lovely bi-blue Sheltie who was completely shut down when I met him. He had two bad ear infections, some skin condition on his face, and a load of worms (hooks, whips, and rounds). No wonder he was so shut down; he must have been in a lot of pain!

At home, Gavin was basically a house ornament. He just lay in a corner or hid under the bed. I didn't know how to reach him. Once outside, Gavin never wanted to come back in, which was my biggest problem. Gavin had to learn that he was a house dog and not an outside dog, so I hired a trainer for help.

Mainly I learned to let Gavin be Gavin. For a long time, he wouldn't explore; he wouldn't play; he would only move when it was time to go outside. His eyes were dull and lifeless.

Months passed, and one day on a hike Gavin slipped his collar. "Oh, no," I thought, "He is going to run away and never come back!"

But Gavin had no desire to run away, and after that, he became an off-lead hiking dog. Slowly, his ears started to rise, and he finally started taking food from my hand. This was a huge victory! Then one day Gavin discovered that running is fun. And after almost two years, he discovered that playing with my younger dog is fun, too! He was finally a dog: a dog with problems, but a dog nonetheless.

Three years later Gavin still doesn't like to come inside by himself, but a long lead helps with that. He has come out of his shell and now plays and wags his tail. The most delightful thing is that he jumps straight up in the air when he is happy, and he just loves his walks.

Thank God for rescuers and for Gavin. If he hadn't been rescued, he would have been one of the living dead, and despite the challenges we've had, I couldn't imagine life without him.

 *Marcia Cook*

The Mermaid Pool

We live on Phillip Island in Australia, and about 20 years ago I used to go walking with a group of friends and their dogs. A really grotty-looking dog named Magnum regularly used to follow us, playing quite happily with our doggie pack. He looked awful, full of fleas and goodness knows what else. Visiting with him out on our walks was fine, but I certainly didn't want him following me home.

Summer came, and we continued to meet the mangy mutt on the beach. My friends had found out that his owners kept him tied up all day, though obviously he frequently got himself loose. They also discovered that he was being treated badly, though at that time, we were not aware that he was being beaten.

I still didn't want to know anything more about him. As I said, he was just a mess. But Magnum, being the dog he was, persisted. He clearly had other ideas.

One day he followed us home. It was 38 centigrade (about 100 degrees Farenheit), so even though I wouldn't let him in the house, I did give him water. He parked himself on our front lawn; apparently he had decided that we were the family for him.

Unbeknownst to me, Magnum started jumping into our son's room at night. The window was quite high, but to Magnum that wasn't a problem. He and my son became close friends. What could we do? Here was this filthy dog, whom we knew by now was being beaten and starved, and he clearly worshiped our son. We found out where he lived, and my son went 'round there. James asked, "Do you want your dog?"

"No," they said.

"Can I have him?"

"Sure."

And that was that. James brought Magnum home for good. We took him to the vet, where they neutered him and cleaned him up before giving him back to us. "He's about three," they told us.

For better or for worse, we had another dog. Magnum wasn't a bit surprised about it, as he had decided to adopt us weeks earlier. He was just keeping busy working out how to make us see it.

Magnum was on his best behavior from day one. He watched our German Shepherd to learn the house rules.

"Sit," I said.

I can do that, he showed me.

"Drop," I said.

No problem, was his silent reply.

We soon realized what a nice dog Magnum was, especially now that he had put on some weight and his coat was starting to shine. The only problem he had was that he would attack anyone working with anything that looked like a stick (vacuum cleaner and garden tools included). His family must have beaten him badly with stick-like objects, but gradually we taught him that he had nothing to fear.

He lived with us until the ripe old age of 20. During those many years, he became my husband's dog; they really bonded. Even so, Magnum was always his own "man." He was attacked once by a Pit Bull and once by a Rottie, but he came off best both times. No one man or beast was ever going to hurt him again.

Magnum would go walkabout (an Aboriginal expression). He would just check that all was well with his neighborhood and then come home again. It wasn't until he died that I realized how he had looked after our property. There were no rabbits or snakes on his watch. After Magnum died, many rabbits and a few snakes rejoiced.

My husband died six months after Magnum. We put their ashes together and scattered them in The Mermaid Pool, a large, deep, rock-rimmed pool only accessible at low tide. They loved each other so much that I find solace in thinking of them together when I walk on the beach.

Yep, Magnum sure was a great dog, and I'm so glad he adopted us.

 *Christine Caldwell*

The Life Every Dog Should Have

It all started when I was scrolling through an online classified site. I normally just conduct a search by typing "Collie" in the search bar, but on this day I had extra time and decided to scroll through all the ads. When an ad entitled "Dog Left To Die" caught my attention, I clicked on it.

The ad was posted by a concerned citizen. It said this person had observed a Collie standing beside the road for days waiting for his owners to return. They had obviously dumped him. The dog was mangy and emaciated. The observer said the abandoners should be ashamed of themselves for leaving such a devoted, loyal, forgiving dog to fend for himself. She also said that several times she had tried to catch the dog, but each time he ran off whenever she got close.

I emailed the poster to find out the specifics. She was very kind and was concerned for the dog, stating that she wasn't optimistic that he had survived the terrible storms we had had the night before because she had not seen him since.

I emailed her back and told her that most strays will come out of hiding in the early morning or late evening hours when it is cooler. At 8:00 that night, she replied to say she had seen him again on a different street, but he was obviously on the move now looking for food.

This was wonderful news. Now we knew he was still alive. Within a half hour, two other Houston Collie Rescue volunteers and I came up with a plan to meet the next morning and scour the neighborhood.

When we gathered, we decided to troll the neighborhood in one vehicle. We turned down the street where he was last seen. I looked on one side while Barb and Virginia searched the other side. All of a sudden, Virginia spotted the dog standing in an empty lot. We got out of the car, and, of course, the dog took off running. I went straight toward him while Virginia and Barb came at him from the very far side of the lot. I offered him canned dog food on a plate, and Barb suggested that I call him Laddie. (For some reason, everyone names their Collies "Laddie" or "Lassie.")

I started telling him what a wonderful, pretty, precious boy he was. Then I sat on the ground with the food at arm's length and kept calling him in my happy baby voice. When he came as close as a foot away, he slinked down to the ground and crawled to the plate on his belly. I was then able to gently touch the top of his head with one hand while stealthily slipping the leash over his head with the other. Once he finished eating, he pranced to the car by my side. I was almost in tears.

This was my first stray dog rescue, and I know they won't always be that easy. This Collie was tired of running and so hungry that I think he was ready to be caught. He gave us all Collie kisses before we loaded him into the kennel for the ride to Virginia's house, where he would be fostered.

I believe it was God's will that we rescued this baby. Why did I scroll through the ads instead of narrowing my search that day? Why was it so easy to catch him when the kind citizen couldn't?

We named him Ryan. He will have to complete heartworm treatment before he is adopted, but we will see him through that. The important thing is that from that day on, Ryan was safe and ensured the life that every dog should have.

 Angela Walker

Long Tails Short

Two-fer: After seeing his profile online, I tried to meet Roddy in person at an adoption event. Roddy wasn't there, but I did meet two very friendly volunteers: Jessica and Jack. Jack did my home visit, which is part of the adoption process. It was only supposed to take 30 minutes but ended up being two hours long; we were having such a great time! Soon thereafter, I adopted Roddy, who quickly made it his job to be my protector and bed-hogger. Adopting this cuddly companion and exercise partner was a great choice, and I got a two-fer: Jack and I started dating! We have now been together for more than two years, and I owe it all to my Border Collie, Roddie. He saved me from my solitude and brought me to Petsmart that day where I met Jack. Matchmaker and savoir, that's my Roddy! -*Audrey Campbell*

Sovereign Sheltie: When one dog goes to the Rainbow Bridge, the only way I can seem to recover is to bring a new one into my life. When my Chow, who had been with me for 12 years, passed away, my husband suggested we foster a Sheltie. I agreed, and we were able to help the rescue take in Princess just before her number was up at the shelter. She was calm, thin, and too tall for a Sheltie. The rescue put her picture on their website and immediately began taking calls from people who wanted to adopt her, but my husband, who was a cat person when we married, said, "She's such a wonderful dog; I think we should adopt her ourselves." We did, and Princess reigned over our home and our hearts during her 12 years with us. -*Mickey Brown*

Treat Every Mistake

Once I graduated college and was officially settled, I decided that I really wanted to get a dog (a *rescue* dog, to be exact). And the breed that I had always loved was the Border Collie. I had pet-sat for a Border Collie while in college and just fell in love with that dog's personality, intelligence, and work ethic. It was a good fit for my lifestyle, so I began hitting the humane societies, Petfinder.com, and Border Collie rescue websites looking for a dog who struck my fancy. Finally I came across Blue Ridge Border Collie Rescue

(BRBCR) in Virginia. Their website was very informative and featured each adoptable dog prominently.

There were a few challenges, though. First, I live in Florida, and BRBCR requires a home inspection as part of their adoption qualification process. Second, this would be my first dog, and because Border Collies tend to be overwhelming for the unprepared, the rescue prefers applications from people with more dog experience. Nevertheless, after hours of discussion with Sylvia, a BRBCR foster mom, and another volunteer from the humane society in Florida who agreed to perform my home inspection on behalf of BRBCR, I was cleared to adopt Westley.

Westley was categorized by Sylvia as a "starter" Border Collie. He was saved from a kill shelter in West Virginia by BRBCR and was a bit more subdued than the average high-drive Border Collie. What he was, in fact, was incredibly shut down and scared from his shelter experience. Sylvia suggested that I try dog agility with him, since agility gives dogs an opportunity to run and play and gain confidence, which can carry over to other aspects of their lives. I agreed, and off we went to baby agility class.

It turned out that Westley loved agility, especially the treats. He was a quick study, eager to please and even more eager to be rewarded. What he was not too pleased about was the instructor's brand of training – repetitive – requiring him to do the same sequences over and over again. As a result, Westley began to shut down again, I was stricken. I had no idea why my dog, who had been showing such potential, would all of a sudden be moving more and more slowly. I sought solutions and found a different trainer, one who was all about the fun, which kept our lessons from becoming tedious and boring. West picked back up, and although he was never going to be the fastest dog out there, at least he wasn't walking the course anymore.

We entered our first agility trial without any expectations. He was either going to have fun or take his place as my ottoman warrior. To my delight, he ran and looked like he was having a good time, just enough not to afford himself permanent retirement. But he was still too slow to have a qualifying run. I knew we would have to spend more time figuring out what motivated Westley, or he would not be fast enough to be an agility dog at the higher levels. I again sought solutions, this time from a friend who saw the potential in Westley and suggested that I actually start giving him treats for making a mistake, in essence, rewarding mistakes to let him know they weren't the end of the world. It worked! He started gaining confidence and running faster and faster.

I was very excited about Westley's new enthusiasm until his past again crept up to haunt him. We were at the beach one day, and West, who thinks that water is a terrible thing, was in a crate when a truck drove by with a flapping tarp. The sound of the tarp scared Westley so badly that he shook intensely and seemed unable to even see me trying to comfort him. I don't want to think what he would have done if he hadn't been in a crate; mentally he was "gone," and the crate was the only thing keeping him physically present. That one moment of fear pervaded all aspects of his life; from then on, every noise set him into flight.

I knew that I had to work through this with him not just for his agility career, but for his quality of life. Again we reverted to the old "treat every mistake" idea, and I began giving him a treat when a door slammed, a dog ran through a tunnel, or a flag blew in the breeze. Slowly he started to come back. We didn't push it; we went in, did three jumps, and then left, so that Westley would feel successful before becoming afraid. He got better and better until he would only *notice* the teeter slamming in the next ring, as opposed to running from it.

It was not until years later when I was at a humane society that I finally figured out why the tarp triggered such a response in Westley. It was the same sound as the wheels of the bins, which were used to move puppies around the shelter, when they rolled over the floor grates. When he heard that noise, poor Westley was transported back to his past.

I adopted Westley nearly seven years ago, and through all the trials, troubles, and triumphs, one thing remains constant: Westley is a survivor. He has taught me never to give up and to find a solution no matter how unusual it may seem. He showed me that there is never only one way to do anything and that the reward for perseverance can come in the form of a little, rescued dog who has exceeded expectations and defied all the odds to become a multiple agility dog champion.

Westley is now retired from three venues (CPE, NADAC, and USDAA), not because he decided that running agility was not fun or that it was too stressful, but because he earned the highest titles that those venues have to offer. He does, however, continue to run in the AKC and is working on his fourth championship. Each time I think he might want to retire to his ottoman, he begins to run faster and with more confidence.

He is truly an inspiration for the underdog. The key is for us humans to simply to find the right buttons to push.

Westley's story is all about perseverance and giving the most unlikely candidate a chance. BRBCR gave me, an unproven dog owner from Florida, a chance to get a Border Collie and become involved in a sport that changed my life. Westley got the chance to exceed expectations and achieve things that most dogs never even come close to in the sport of agility. He also got the chance to show the world that no matter how you come to your forever home and with whatever baggage you are carrying, you can succeed and find happiness.

 *Gill Chapman*

Hidden Genius

My husband and I first started searching for our second dog after having such success with our other rescue dog, Lucy. Lucy is part Welsh Corgi and part Golden Retriever, a funny but adorable combination. We got her when she was eight weeks old, and while we loved the "puppy experience," we wanted a dog who was a little bit older this time around.

We found one listed on Petfinder.com by Western Border Collie Rescue (WBCR) who was part Welsh Corgi and part Border Collie. She was the perfect age, so we applied. Adoption approval took some time, and by the time we were able to adopt, she had already been adopted. At the time, we were in the midst of wedding planning, so we put our dog hunt on the back burner until the wedding was over. This gave us some time to think, and my husband became concerned that bringing another dog into the house might ruin our relationship with Lucy.

I knew we already had a good thing going, but I also thought Lucy would benefit from having a playmate. I put WBCR on the hunt to find us the perfect dog, and a couple weeks later they contacted us with a match: a 10-month-old dog named Aiden, who was currently being fostered by a woman named Barb in Fort Collins.

My husband, Lucy, and I made the hour-long trek to Fort Collins to meet Aiden. He was an orange color, which Barb explained was the result of his being left outside all the time and being fed poor-quality food. He seemed fairly subdued. At some point Aiden had landed in a high-kill shelter with a leg injury. WBCR took him into their care and rehabilitated his injury. I fell in love with him immediately but was concerned because his personality was so different from Lucy's; I didn't know if he could keep up with her.

Despite my concerns, we decided to take Aiden home. Renamed Jake, our new dog struggled through his first two weeks in our home. Lucy and Jake would "play fight" a little too aggressively, and Jake would growl at Lucy every time she went near a toy, bone, or person he fancied. I lost many nights of sleep wondering if we had made the right decision. What did Jake really want and need? Since we couldn't be around the dogs all day long, I fretted constantly while at work, too. Was rescuing a dog the wrong choice?

Our Border Collie research said that the breed was genius in nature, easily figuring out things like how to open doors. We had hoped that perhaps our new dog could learn to wash dishes, too! But what we got instead was, well, Jake. Before bringing Jake home, we had secured all of our doors and purchased as many "genius" toys as we could find to keep him safe and busy all day long. When we presented him with one of the toys for the first time expecting him to catch right on and entertain himself for hours, he looked at it with such disinterest that I felt a horrible pain in my stomach. I couldn't help my disappointment: this dog seemed to have none of the Border Collie traits about which we had read. He fumbled with stairs, ran into doors, and couldn't follow a tossed ball. He was so clumsy that I took him to the vet thinking that maybe his eyesight was bad. (It wasn't.)

The first two weeks turned into a month. The month turned into two, and then three, and then six... But now it seems as though the transformation happened overnight. Feeding Jake the right diet, giving him the right amount of exercise, and letting him be the indoor/outdoor dog he wanted to be has turned him into the real Border Collie of our dreams. His coat is now a beautiful, dark auburn color, and his Border Collie traits shine through. It's a rare occurrence for me not to be "herded" down our stairs. He knows our walk routine. If I don't make the exact left over the bridge where we normally go, he stops and looks at me as if to say, "Mom, you're not going the right way!"

When I pick him up from doggie daycare, they tell me, "There were a lot of dogs here today, and Jake didn't appreciate how untidy they were, so he herded them all together."

As for Jake and Lucy, they're best friends. When I have to take one of them somewhere that the other one can't go, it's as if I ripped their hearts out. Jake originally struggled with separation anxiety when my husband and I traveled out of town. He always lost weight. But this most recent time, at the Doggie Dude Ranch, Jake did just fine! No weight loss whatsoever. My husband said, "Maybe he got used to it there."

I looked down at Jake sleeping in my lap and said, "No, I think he's just finally figured out that we're *always* going to pick him up and bring him home."

Did we make the right decision about adopting Jake? Absolutely. I don't know what his life was like before he came to be with us, but I'm sure glad that he picked us for his forever home. Jake's been the most wonderful, amazing, life-changing dog for us. It took me a while to realize that the only key necessary to open the door to Jake's true personality and underlying "genius" was our unconditional love.

 Courtney Teasdale and Ryan Katapski

The Power of Love

I first saw Rollo, a handsome Corgi boy, on a Texas Corgi rescue group website. He had been abandoned and lost in downtown Denton, Texas, at the age of about eight. He was blind, heartworm-positive, mangy, emaciated (only 14 pounds!), and diabetic. The rescue group took him in, fed him, treated his mange, stabilized his diabetes, and posted him on their website for adoption.

My own Corgi, Abbey Rose, was in the market for a companion. My cancer treatments were finally complete, and I was planning to return to work, so it seemed logical for Abbey to have a friend to play with each day while I was gone. I was committed to finding the perfect rescue dog, and it would soon be Rollo. For whatever reason, his photo and special needs called out to me. I went back to his web posting again and again for weeks just to look at this special boy.

They say love makes you blind to another's imperfections and flaws. It makes you lose all practicality, which is what happened to me. After discovering that Rollo had been in rescue for six months with nobody expressing any interest in adopting him, I shifted my idea of adopting him into high gear and quickly brought him home.

I've only become a dog person during the last year, so taking on a blind dog requiring insulin injections was unfamiliar territory. But love can create denial of any challenges by helping one see them as lessons and opportunities instead. Such was the case for me.

A few things I learned right away. For example, I quickly came to know that those without vision possess a keen sense of hearing. Rollo could hear everything inside and outside the house. He could hear car doors shutting, keys jingling, and dogs barking down the street. He could also hear me preparing his meal twice each day, including the sound of the pantry door opening and the can opener being removed from the drawer. He was an auditory wizard!

Not untypical for an abandoned dog left to fend for himself, food was a real priority for this little man. He would eat every meal as if he were in a race, but over time, what started as aggression turned into celebration. I called his incessant, meal-related barking and jumping "The Rollo Dance." And I learned that the best way to keep this "dance" under control was to prepare his insulin *before* prepping his food.

That became another lesson for me. I've never given anyone a shot, but our veterinarian taught me a simple trick for insulin injections: do it was while the dog is eating. Rollo never flinched, never growled. Somehow he knew I would never hurt him. Rollo trusted me with all his heart, and I hope I never betrayed that trust.

You might think a blind dog would develop a strong sense of dependence because his world was always dark as night, but not Rollo. He was a strong-willed guy who quickly learned how to get around on his own. Abbey was a wonderful guide in the beginning, helping him navigate the house, the back yard, and down the street for walks. In time, Rollo learned the course and could make it on his own.

One of my favorite memories was our first visit to the puppy park. Rollo had probably not been in such a vast space to roam in a long time, not to mention the stimulation of being with so many other dogs. While he was almost twice as big as Abbey, Rollo remained right by her side, following her to the right, the left, wherever else she chose to wander. It was a touching moment to watch them both; Abbey knowing that she was his eyes, Rollo knowing that Abbey was to be trusted.

Rollo was terribly afraid of thunder. I was known to leave in the middle of a meeting if I was needed to rescue his nerves from an unexpected storm. Isn't that what a parent does? I never wanted him to be afraid, certainly not afraid *and alone*. In the beginning, his entire body would shake with fear while he lay on top of me. I would rub him and speak softly in his ears. As time passed, he no longer would shake, even though he still preferred to perch on top of my body, where he knew he was safe.

Sadly, Rollo's health eventually took a turn for the worse, especially the diabetes, and he passed away from this world to cross the Rainbow Bridge. Two days later, I was awakened around one o'clock in the morning by a big clap of thunder. Instinctively, I jumped from my bed and immediately called for Rollo. It took a few seconds to remember he was no longer here. I sat on the sofa and cried. And I kept crying, missing my little man, my gentleman Corgi, until I remembered that people like me believe there is a special place for our beloved dogs, something like Dog Heaven, and that's where Rollo is. Surely, now, his sweet soul no longer has to endure thunderstorms or insulin shots. And maybe he now has sight and can see everything before him. Oh, I hope so; it is what I chose to believe.

I kept Rollo's collar. It was a special collar that I purchased just for him to honor his sweet soul. It has a small, brass tag on it that reads: "A dog is the only thing on earth that loves you more than he loves himself."

That was surely my Rollo.

This special-needs pup certainly changed my life. I will forever miss him and always feel privileged that he blessed my home with his unconditional love for all who entered.

Farewell Rollo. We'll be together soon when we meet at the Rainbow Bridge.

 *Stacy Sells*

Fish Flop Foster

I n a total rush as usual, between family, work, and animal rescue, I made my way to the local animal shelter on my lunch break, just as I had promised. I'd read a plea on Facebook the night before for an arthritic Shih Tzu who needed to be rescued quickly to avoid euthanasia. As I walked through the doors and heard the sounds of the dogs from the back kennel area, I was told by the receptionist that the Shih Tzu had just left with another rescue. Filled with a sense of relief, I thought (as most rescuers do), "On to the next one in need!"

I walked past the kennels and couldn't help but notice the most handsome Blue Heeler I'd ever seen. There sat Rossi, quiet and alone, looking as if his spirit were broken.

I've found that bringing the mixed breeds into our Alabama SPCA rescue program and sending the purebreds to breed-specific rescues helps us save the most lives. Therefore, I made a mental note to ask what, if any, plans had been made for the Heeler.

To my surprise, the rescue coordinator asked if I wanted him and told me to take him because he was stressed by all the noise. I excitedly grabbed a slip lead and headed over to wrangle up my newest rescue. After all, I knew I could find this boy an awesome breed-specific rescue that would help him transition to a permanent home.

After nearly 15 minutes of the best-looking dog in the entire shelter flopping like a fish and submissively urinating and defecating, I decided that walking him out wasn't going to work. I didn't turn around to see the looks on the workers' faces as I carried Rossi to my car. He seemed scared stiff, but that was understandable, since he had been languishing in that run for nine days since his owner had surrendered him.

The next few months proved to be a whirlwind. Rossi had all the necessities to feel right at home, including a large doghouse, cedar shavings, and a soft bed in the largest outside kennel I owned. For the first few weeks, anytime I approached to feed Mr. Handsome, he would make circles in the kennel, letting go of his bladder and bowels the entire time. I'd never seen anything like it. Some days it seemed we took two steps forward and then three back.

One thing I knew for sure was that either I'd have to work really hard for a long time to earn Handsome's trust, or we needed a rescue commitment quick. This boy was going to be a challenge. I networked through Facebook and email, sharing beautiful pictures of this scared dog and his bio: a victim of divorce, never socialized, apparently purchased as a yard ornament by someone oblivious to the needs of the Cattle Dog breed.

After receiving no offers of help from breed-specific rescues, I decided that this dog would be my own personal challenge. Maybe a rescue could later help me place him into a forever home, once we got some of his issues worked out. But I made a commitment when I carried him from the shelter to my car the day I rescued him. Rossi needed a clean slate. His owner had thrown him away and broken his delicate heart.

I knew just what to do. First, a new name. Handsome's namesake would have to be a strong, resilient, Crimson Tide football player. I thought of their running back, Jalston Fowler, and renamed my stunningly good-looking boy Jalston. For a while he heard his new name a lot because I wanted him to forget his previous name and life so that we could start moving forward. And move forward inch-by-inch he did! Jalston started opening up more after being around a very outgoing dog and seeing her interact with me. If I sat down, he would come to me for a quick pat on the head. But that was all, nothing else! Jalston was still scared of the lead, and it took him more than a month to leave his kennel, which occurred on Thanksgiving day.

I don't know that any of my company actually understood my excitement that day. Not only was I thankful for family, friends, and the simple things in life, but my bashful rescue had achieved a major accomplishment. I knew he had wanted to come outside the kennel, but his fear was holding him back. It was the biggest step forward we had taken to date, and from there we were off like a rocket. In the coming weeks, I would learn just how smart this Cattle Dog really was.

As the Christmas holidays approached, I spent a lot of time at home cleaning, decorating, and preparing. Jalston learned to trust me. He looked forward to mealtime, when he would sit and wait patiently for his food. I couldn't believe the progress we'd made. We still had a ways to go, but we were off to a great start. Jalston still needed to learn what it was like to be inside with the family, and he definitely needed to meet more people.

No other gift could have been better than the one I received Christmas Eve, 10 weeks after rescuing Jalston. I left the carport door open, and, believe it or not, the curious Cattle Dog made his way inside! Once in, I shut the door and secured him in a wire crate with a soft blanket. We reached a huge milestone that night, with Jalston sleeping inside for probably the first time in his life. Jalston quietly watched the other dogs mingle with us until he fell asleep. It was probably the best sleep he'd ever had.

It's now April, and Jalston has been with us for nearly six months. Through my extensive research, I've learned that Cattle Dogs are extremely intelligent and need jobs to do. The first job I gave Jalston was learning to walk on a leash, and although he still isn't in love with the idea, he's not doing the fish flop like he did six months ago. Jalston has learned to trust me. Most importantly, he now sees that we humans aren't all uncaring and cruel. He knows he has a forever friend in me, no matter what.

Jalston will remain with me until the perfect forever home for him is found. Any experienced Cattle Dog fan looking for a handsome, hopeful new project? Call me!

 *Shannon Walker*

Long Tails Short

Three's a Company: Cattle Dogs may be a bit thick-headed, but what do you expect from a dog who is bred to be kicked in the head and keep going? We live on a 700-acre cattle ranch, and we decided to add a bigger, older dog to our family, both for protection and to help with the cows, we knew a Cattle Dog would be perfect. Enter Murray. In the beginning, he and our other two dogs scuffled a bit, but they eventually worked it out; now they are best friends. These days Murray's area of concern encompasses us all. He doesn't bother our chickens and has just started to figure out his relationship to the horses. Murry is just what we were looking for. We feel protected instead of threatened, and we look forward to enrolling him in herding classes. -*Victoria Capaci*

Who Needs Trees? Kirby, a thin, white-faced, weather-worn, Sheltie, was found tethered to a shed alongside a desolate stretch of highway in Northwest Pennsylvania. The first thing this blind, deaf dog did when he got out of the rescue transport vehicle was to cock his leg and pee on his new foster dad's leg (when you are blind, anything vertical will work). This christening was the beginning of a love affair. Kirby has been in our home for a year and a half. His blindness and deafness do not stop the joy in his soul. He spins in circles in our yard, barking with glee. The vet does not understand how an old boy with a grade four heart murmur is thriving, but we know the secret is lots of love and Mom's homemade dog food. Kirby is a grateful soul, but no one is more grateful than us humans. This old boy and his pack of old, "forever foster" Shelties fill our home with love...and lots of hairballs! -*Nancy Van Horn*

Guilty as Charged

Thisis love story isn't about Match.com or eHarmony; it's about a search to find a replacement for my beloved dog, Rooster, who stayed behind in my previous home when I moved out.

At first, I thought I wanted a Sheltie who could match Rooster's wit, beauty, and tenacious courage. My search took me to every Sheltie rescue website within a reasonable distance and then beyond, but nothing in those cute little faces or poignant stories made me want *that* dog. Strangely, as I continued my search, I found myself drawn to Border Collies.

As my interest in and knowledge of Border Collies grew, so did my desire to adopt one, which led me to the Blue Ridge Border Collie Rescue site. I read profile after profile of cute little puppies, working dogs, and old dogs who just needed some love, but none struck me until I read about Maxx.

Maxx was almost three years old and considered to be a "project dog" by trainer Sally Williams, who was fostering him. The reason he was considered "special" is that he had been let out of his kennel so infrequently that he was sleeping in his own waste. He was a true rescue; they had to shave off all his hair to let the blisters on his skin heal. As you can imagine, Maxx knew very little about how to socialize with humans or even other dogs. Tears ran down my face as I read his description, and even now it strikes a soft spot deep in my heart to think about my beautiful, intelligent Buckshot being treated that way.

After trading a few emails with Sally, I submitted my adoption form and waited for an answer. I was apprehensive because, at the time, I lived in a tiny 390-square-foot condo with nothing more than a wraparound porch to call a fenced-in yard. After the requisite home visit, I sat on pins and needles for a day or so before receiving adoption approval and an appointment time to meet Maxx.

The big day came, and I was so sure I was going to adopt Maxx that I stopped and bought a big kennel for him at Tractor Supply on my way. After I arrived and talked to Sally for a bit, she took me to the big pen in the yard where Maxx was kept along with a few other dogs. I could tell right away that Maxx was going to be a handful because he was wearing a muzzle. The meeting was not quite what I had planned, and Maxx was much bigger than I had anticipated. He almost knocked me off my feet when he came running to greet this new person in the pen. I have to give the boy credit for enthusiasm! I really don't remember much more about that first visit other than the excitement of finally meeting and adopting Maxx.

One thing that has remained vividly ingrained in my mind is how overwhelmed I felt at the prospect of turning this seemingly uncontrollable bundle of fur into an obedient, contributing member of my one-man household. More than once I looked back at Maxx in the kennel and wondered if I had finally bitten off more than I could chew. His face told me I could do it; my heart told me the same, but my mind screamed at the impracticality of keeping a dog of his size and energy level in such a small apartment. I would need to take Maxx for several *long* walks each day. Where would I find the time?

First, we needed a name change. There's nothing wrong with Maxx, but he just didn't look like a Maxx to me. All of the black dots on his white front legs gave me the idea to call him Buckshot. I was surprised at how quickly he came to know his name, and I truly believe that a new name from his new human began the important bonding process for his training. I won't go on and on about the early days – the chewed up footwear, the inevitable messes on the carpet – but I will restate that this dog was more than a handful. He was, indeed, a full-fledged project. Buckshot's first toy frog lasted all of about 10 minutes.

Surprisingly, it didn't take long for us to figure each other out. I think Buckshot knew early on that all I wanted was to love him and help him reach his full potential as a great dog. Long, frequent walks as spring began to look like summer helped build a bond between us, and we started to develop trust. One afternoon in mid-June, I decided to see if the trust was warranted by letting Buckshot off his leash. The lump in my throat turned to lead as he took off like a shot with no apparent intention, whatsoever, of coming back. At least not in my lifetime. He knew where he lived, and he knew where his food came from, so I wasn't totally worried that he'd be gone forever. We lived on the side of a mountain where few people and even fewer cars ever ventured. Lots of dogs ran free there, so he wouldn't be in much danger; at least, that's what I rationalized.

As I had hoped, Buckshot showed up at home an hour later, looking for all the world like nothing untoward had just happened. I let him go; he went; he came back. I could tell he enjoyed it, so over the summer, I found ways to let him go free without being tempted to run away. When the leash came off, he had a job to do - fetch the tennis ball for me. This wasn't an ordinary fetch the tennis ball game, though. No, this was "jump in the creek and retrieve the tennis ball." It was the kind of task that kept him from turning into a porch potato, wore him out, and gave him a sense of accomplishment. We spent the next month doing this, until I figured out that the organisms in the water were responsible for his runny stool. That was a good reason to stop, and by then he had learned to come to me whenever I called, and he never ran out of earshot again.

The rest of the story is now very much like most "normal" relationships between a man and his Border Collie. Buckshot is tremendously loyal and has become an obedient, happy dog who gets into trouble only when he isn't challenged and worked often enough to suit him, which means two or three times a day. The only serious problem he has is what I'm guessing is separation anxiety. I used to take him everywhere I went, weather appropriate. He knows what "truck ride" means, and he's always ready to go. The back seat used to be his spot, but now he just rides where the back seat used to be. That's because he chewed the whole thing up, and I had to take it to the dump.

I have since been reunited with Rooster, and my two dogs are now constant companions. They love to play together.

Speaking of dump, Buckshot is not without a sense of humor. I got back to the truck one day after a shopping errand, only to find a pile of doggie doo-doo in my seat. Since Rooster sits in the front and Buckshot in the back, I started yelling at Rooster, telling him what a bad dog he was. Then I noticed the size of the "deposit" and realized that it could not be Rooster's. Buckshot had jumped into the front seat, left me a present, and then returned to the back seat, all in the space of five minutes. After figuring out what had happened, all I could do was laugh and apologize to Rooster for scolding him. I knew there was a reason that Border Collies always look guilty... Because they are!

 *Curt Harvey*

Breaking the Silence

I remember the moment I knew she would be mine. I had driven an hour to pick her up from a home where she no longer fit in. She sat on the seat next to me. For the entire ride home, she stared at my face. She was searching for answers. Who was I? Where was she going? What would become of the life she had known, and what was to come for her now? Stopped at a traffic light, I returned her stare. She looked deep into my soul, and I saw all her questions. There was so much more to life than she had been allowed to experience. I was hooked.

Grace started out life just like any other happy puppy. But it soon became apparent that she wasn't like other puppies.

She was deaf. Her original family had fallen in love with her puppy cuteness but was not prepared for this surprise. As she grew older and started doing normal, naughty puppy things, they struggled to communicate with her. Grace spent many hours each day in a crate. When she was given freedom out of her crate, her family had to chase her and catch her to put her back in the crate. This taught her that a person reaching for her was a bad thing and that she should run the other way.

As Grace got older and became a teenage puppy, she began to bark in her crate from lack of stimulation. The neighbors complained. Reluctantly, the family called Northern Chesapeake Sheltie Rescue (NCSR) to find her a new home.

Grace's first weeks with me were quite challenging. She barked, she pooped and peed on my floor, she chewed my plants, and she would not allow me to touch her. She would not walk on a leash, ascend or descend stairs, or pass through any doorways at all, even to follow my other dogs in or out. She was not cooperative with grooming procedures. She ran wildly through the house and yard whenever I gave her freedom and refused to come back to me. She did not play with toys or chew on bones. I had to start over with her from square one.

I tried to get her attention with treats. Most of them she would not even take from my hand. She just sniffed and then turned her nose away, refusing to acknowledge that it was even there. The few that she did take from my hand she ran away with and spit out on the floor (the other dogs were thrilled about this!). Every day, many times a day, I'd try to hand her tiny goodies, and at the end of each day, I'd feel like I had failed. Finally, after a week, I found one food that she would eat consistently from my hand. Now I had something to work with to get her attention.

Each time I touched Grace, she got a treat. I made sure to touch her many times throughout the day when I was not going to take away her freedom and put her in a crate. I didn't want her to associate me touching her with being locked up again. Of course, there were times when I needed to use the crate to ensure her safety when I couldn't watch her, but I gave her as much freedom at other times as I could. Slowly, she stopped flinching and bracing herself when I reached for her. She learned to tolerate brushing and nail trimming. She learned that it was safe to walk in and out of doorways by following my other dogs out to the yard, where she had a safe place to run and play.

I used a treat to lure her into a sit over and over again. After several days, she started to offer a sit on her own when she saw the treat. She was so proud of herself! She would sit, eat her treat, and then run circles happily around the room before coming back and sitting in front of me for another treat. She was so happy to finally know what was expected and to have a way to communicate with someone in her life! Then I added the sign language signal for sit. It took a bit longer for Grace to respond only to the hand signal without a treat, but once she did, she showed her pride again by running in circles around the room or yard. The silence had been broken! We had developed a way to communicate with each other.

Now that I had reached her, Grace started watching me closely. I used sign language with her every day to communicate both silly little things and major life events. She learned signs for her daily activities like going outside, receiving toys and bones, getting a drink, eating meals, going for a walk, etc. She also learned silly signs like naughty girl, pretty, silly, playtime, night-night, etc. I signed to her about everything. It was like a pool of knowledge had been opened up to her, and she was drinking in every word.

I am amazed at how quickly Grace picks up new signs. Sometimes she recognizes them after seeing them only once or twice. She watches me very closely and seems to thrive on learning new things. This has also taught me how to be aware of my body language and emotions. Grace is so much more aware of my subtle movements and my state of energy than my other dogs. While they are also aware, they tend to fall back on my verbal communication to them to know what to do. Conversely, Grace is always aware and will often start to do things even before the sign is given simply because she notices the subtlest cues that come before the sign.

Grace is a joy to have in our lives. Everyone who meets her falls immediately in love with her. They stoop down and call her to them. When I explain that she can't hear them calling, they are always so sad. Some back away from her as if she has something horribly wrong and contagious. It upsets me to see people perceive her differently just because she can't hear.

The lucky people who take the time to ask questions and get to know Grace are amazed by her normalcy. They are surprised that she gets along wonderfully with my dogs who can hear. Anyone who sees us working together in obedience and agility is always inspired to work a bit harder with their own dogs.

Grace has found her place here with us, and I cannot imagine our home without her now.

 *Debbie Bauer*

Just to Look

I grew up with both a father and a grandfather who were veterinarians, so, of course, I love all animals. I have had Cattle Dogs my entire life and can't imagine it without them. God blessed us when he created these wonderful, loyal, loving dogs.

After losing my childhood dogs to old age and realizing how empty my life was without them, I got another little Blue Heeler named Ellie from an old farmer when she was just six months old. She lived to be 17½ years old and was a huge part of me. I was so sad to lose her, but the memory of the many of joy I had with her reminds me that I was lucky.

Here's where my rescue volunteer story begins. After Elli passed, I knew I wanted to get another dog, but I never thought it would be just three weeks later. I had found New Hope Cattle Dogs Rescue and Rehoming of Colorado's website and had visited it many times. One day they were advertising an adoption event in Golden, Colorado, and we decided to go, "just to look."

There were lots of wonderful dogs at the adoption event. Though I was still heartbroken, there was a specific deaf dog, Bounce, whom I had seen on the website and couldn't get out of my mind. I was hoping to see her that day, but she wasn't there. That's when we met Wrangler, a gorgeous, blue, loving dog, who decided that we were to be his humans.

My husband and I spent a little time with Wrangler away from the other dogs just to get to know him. New Hope told us he was heartworm-positive, and they were paying for his treatments. Our plan was to think it over and get my father's professional opinion about the heartworms before we made any decisions, but I wanted to make sure New Hope knew we were interested. I didn't want anyone else to adopt Wrangler out from under us!

Upon hearing our plan, New Hope suggested we foster Wrangler with the intention of adopting him. I had never considered fostering and didn't know much about the process before the event, but my husband and I immediately agreed.

As soon as Wrangler hopped in the car, we were in love with him. No way were we just going to foster him and then find him a new home; we were going to be his forever family, no matter what. When we took him for a follow-up on his heartworms, we discovered he was still positive. New Hope paid for further expensive treatment and even allowed us to take Wrangler to our veterinarian of choice.

Treating heartworm is a painful and sometimes lethal process for dogs to endure, so we were happy to be able to have our own vet care for Wrangler. During that time, we had to keep him "quiet" so that the dying worms wouldn't clot in his lungs. As you can imagine, that wasn't the easiest thing, but Wrangler took it like a champ. After several months, we finally got the all-clear that the heartworms were gone. I cannot thank our vet and New Hope enough for saving his life.

I don't know what Wrangler's life was like before he came to live with us. People say we rescued him, but we feel like he rescued us from broken hearts. If you have never owned a Cattle Dog or a herding-breed dog, you are truly missing out on one of God's greatest creatures. They are incredibly intelligent, loyal dogs. They can be trained to do just about anything, and their hard-working, high-energy nature makes them perfect for dog sports like agility. I believe they have the biggest hearts of any breed, and the bond between Cattle Dogs and their humans is very strong.

After experiencing the rescue and rehabilitation process with Wrangler, we couldn't help but get more involved with New Hope. We even began fostering dogs. It's been incredibly rewarding to help these dogs get a second chance at a happy, healthy, love-filled life.

 Lisa O'Sullivan

From Litter Boxes to Long Walks

B efore you came into my life with your four large paws, floppy ears, wet kisses, table-clearing tail, and glossy, penguin-like coat, I considered myself a confirmed cat person. "Cat people," as we are known by the masses, enjoy the feline faculties such as an inherently independent nature, the desire to defecate in a small box that deftly conceals the evidence, and a lack of demand for vigorous daily exercise. Cats are the pet of choice for those of us unwilling or unable to make long-term emotional commitments. We don't need to rush home to let a cat out to pee. Daily walks are unheard of, and we rarely, if ever, receive a call from a neighbor complaining that our cats' constant meowing is keeping them up at night. "Shut that cat up!" is something I have never heard – not once – in my 30+ years as a self-described cat person.

But I digress. Cats are simple; you are not. The day you arrived I held serious reservations concerning the future of our arrangement together. My son couldn't keep you because you wanted to herd his new baby, and he was afraid you might accidently hurt her. You have to understand that this concern was not completely unreasonable. After all, you should be on a ranch herding sheep, not sequestered in a two-bedroom duplex with wall-to-wall carpeting. What a surprise that he asked me, the woman who harbors a secret Cat Woman fantasy, to adopt you! I don't do dogs; I do cats. You know – tuna, balls of yarn, scratch posts, self-cleaning litter boxes – not bones, squeaky toys, and walks.

Fortunately for you, my life partner is a "dog person," and he suggested that we take you for a short, "trial" week to see how you adapted to our home before taking full-fledged ownership. I know he really meant, "Let's see how the crazy cat lady adapts," but I agreed to try it anyway.

Day one: You lick a lot; this is annoying. Mc-Partner thinks you are sweet and tells me they are kisses, not licks, as if I just landed on Earth, and it is his job to educate me on all things living. You are pretty smart, I'll give you that. One of your Border Collie relatives made the cover of *National Geographic* and was referred to as one of the smartest breeds on the planet. I like that. Better to have a smart dog than a stupid one. I'm impressed with your ability to go to the door and make a low, howling sound to indicate that you need to visit the giant outdoor litter box, and you never mistake any part of the inside of the house for a lawn. You will never fully understand how much this is appreciated.

Week two: After a week of walks, I can't say I'll ever be happy about having to pick up your hot poop with my bare hands (buffered by two double-wrapped Albertson plastic bags, of course); it's disgusting. Would you like to pick up my poop? Just so we have an understanding: Feces is not fun. Mc-Partner agreed at the start that he would "face the feces" in the back yard, which suits me just fine.

Overall I am happy about our walks, though, in that not only do I find people more willing to engage with me while you are in my company, but as a result of our first walking week, I shed about four pounds. This was a surprising externality which is moving me toward the idea that you can stay as my workout partner. You're encouraging but not demeaning, willing to meet my pace, unconcerned about what I'm wearing, and listening attentively to everything I say.

Your arrival came just four months after my mother died. She and I didn't have the best relationship, and I spent most of my life trying to win her love and approval. Upon her death, I realized I had run out of time and needed to cope with the hand I had been dealt.

Toward the end of your trial week, while Mc-Partner is at work and I am parked on my office futon attempting to read, I'm suddenly assaulted with a mishmash of feelings about my mother – some good, some bad – as they spew out from the tightly sealed bottle concealed deep within my emotional pantry. In the background I distantly hear your frantic paw peddling, nails scratching and scraping across the linoleum as you barrel into the room and dive onto the futon.

You use your nose to skillfully pry apart my hands, which are sealed tightly over my eyes as they try to stop the tears from falling. You whimper and force your way through my hand fortress, licking my tears and nuzzling my face, as if to say, "Let me stop the pain. It's okay. *It's okay*!"

I push you down, yet you persist until, finally, I relent. You patiently sit by my side while my body's convulsions slowly dissipate and my mind returns to the here and now.

I've never had a cat do that. Upon any attempt to seek feline consolation, most often I've been met with aloofness or complete rejection. I like this new feeling of being loved, comforted, and not judged. Even the licks, I mean kisses, are nice.

Was my self-described cat-person identity really a projection of the rejection I experienced in my childhood? Could a dog prove to be a more suitable ally than my therapist? Certainly you cost less than the therapist, and I don't have to make an appointment to see you. Plus, my therapist never would dare to cross the professional boundary and give me a hug, let alone lick away my tears. Hmmm, this might just work.

So Katie, you see, I owe you a lot. In just the first few weeks after you came to be with us, you taught me that unconditional love does exist. I learned that it's okay to have poop issues and that I need to walk daily with you because it calms us both. You keep me from hanging out inside my head too much. You ask for very little, but you give so much. I'm indebted to you, girl, for bringing me back to life.

So let's go chase off that Siamese cat who keeps pooping in our garden. Please try and refrain from wanting to eat her poop, as I see a peanut butter snack in your near future.

 *Julie Wian*

Freedom

I am 23 years old, and my dog, Iindey, will soon be six. I adopted her five years ago and named her Iindependence May because she officially became mine just before the Fourth of July. Previously I had been fostering her, but it only took two weeks together for me to know for sure that she was meant to be my dog.

I have struggled with post-traumatic stress disorder (PTSD) since I was young. I am extremely jumpy in crowds, claustrophobic, and challenged to live on my own. Things that are simple for most people, such as going to a bar with friends or out to eat with family, are extremely difficult for me. I have trouble riding the bus, walking in stores, going to the library, and dealing with tasks that are normal and mundane for others. The year before adopting Iindey, I had lost my 16-year-old dog, Ginger, and moved out on my own. These changes made life even more difficult for me. I knew I needed a dog.

As a pet and companion, Iindey didn't have any special "rights" to live with me, and everywhere I tried to rent insisted on no pets or expensive deposits and extra monthly fees. The excessive charges on top of dog food, vet visits, and other necessities were extremely challenging to manage, and Iindey ended up having to stay with my grandmother. This was terrible because at the time, being home with Iindey was the best part of my day.

Today, five years later, I'm currently living with my mom and grandmother because my disabilities have prevented me from keeping my own place. That's all about to change, though, since the ADA (American Disability Act) just updated its guidelines for service animals. I adopted Iindey because I loved her and wanted to give her the best, most spoiled life possible, but now she is more than a pet: she's my service dog. Many of the aforementioned situations that used to cause trouble for me are now less of a problem because Iindey keeps me calm. I drive better with her in the car because I don't panic as easily, and large crowds or people behind me bother me a little less. Iindey watches everything and everyone, which helps me feel safer. She focuses so much on making sure that I am okay that she rarely leaves my side. When I want to cry, Iindey always makes me smile; when I have a vicious nightmare, she jumps on my bed and stretches out beside me to comfort me.

Don't get me wrong, Iindey is still my pet pal, even though her presence helps to keep my life in order, too. I've taught her English, Spanish, and sign language as well as how to get along with cats, horses, and other animals (she's always been great with dogs). But my favorite thing about her is that she is a ball junkie. She'll perpetually bring me the ball if I don't already have it in my hand and then proceed to look between me and the ball, asking if I will throw it for her. Of course, I will!

I needed someone who could see how I was feeling and support me through each day. As you can see, Iindey does all that and more. I can honestly say that she has saved my life too many times to count. I have no idea where I might be without her, and I really don't want to know. At least with her by my side, life is halfway decent, even though sometimes it feels like hell. I thank God every day that I have Iindey; she is the best thing that has ever happened to me since Ginger.

 Alicia Flores

Long Tails Short

Party On: Tori was finally freed from her hell of being chained outside to a trailer, only to be traded into an equally bad situation for a keg of beer. When the libations ran out, so did this girl's time; the boozers dumped her at a shelter where she faced impending euthanasia. When I first saw her, she had occluded eyes, yellow teeth, barely any fur, and an emaciated body at about 30 pounds. I could barely discern species, much less breed or age. When asked if I would foster her, I didn't hesitate. But that only lasted three days before I adopted her. That was years ago. Now, my 10-year-old, 60-pound, clear-eyed, fully-furry, utterly all-puppy Tori Girl loves with all her heart and herds anything and everything in view with her special Collie bark. -*Susan Johnston*

Healing Heelers

"**Y**ou better come get these dogs, or I'm gonna shoot 'em," the caller growled.

Three Blue Heeler (Australian Cattle Dog) puppies had been abandoned on his property. When personnel from M'Shoogy's Emergency Animal Rescue of Savannah, Missouri, found them, the five-month-old sisters were cold, hungry, and terrified of people. Rescuers were only able to capture them because their hunger was more powerful than their fear.

The girls were huddled in a corner of their kennel when Tim and I arrived at the rescue to volunteer. We held them, trying to let them know that humans can be a source of kindness. But the girls had been traumatized by their ordeal. Their little bodies were rigid with fear; in their eyes was a wide-eyed, distant gaze.

But we had hope. We fostered the smallest puppy, Phoenix, first. When Phoenix arrived home, she was afraid of everything – except our dogs. Dakota and Susanna taught Phoenix how to be a normal dog, and Phoenix was a quick study. In just two weeks, she was ready for her forever home with my niece.

While Phoenix was at our house, Tim and I had visited Kristine and Sabrina during our Saturday volunteer sessions. The girls also met other volunteers and the people who brought their food and cleaned their pen, but they were still terrified of humans. Kristine would pace back and forth in her kennel, and Sabrina would stay in a corner until I approached, at which time she would dart away like a frightened rabbit. Kristine seemed to be making some progress, though. At first, she gave me wide berth when she paced past me, but she started to get closer and eventually let me pet her. She would relax a little and let me put her long front legs across my lap, but the clanging of a kennel gate or the banging of a bucket would cause her to jump up and start pacing again.

After Phoenix had gone to her forever home, I returned to the rescue to bring home another puppy. Kristine paced for a while and then let me pet her and hold her a little. Sabrina tried to stay as far away from me as possible. I decided to bring Sabrina home with me first, since she was in such urgent need of socialization.

Sabrina was almost feral. She was terrified of people, and at the slightest sound or movement, she would dart under the printer stand to hide. She was afraid of her food and water dishes, the back door, and even the yard. She firmly refused to go outside. We couldn't take her out on a leash because she had never been walked on a leash before and was terrified of it. When it came time to potty, we had to carry her outside, and when we put her down in the yard, she would scurry off to a corner by the fence. Although she loved our other dogs and interacted with them, she was not as quick to emulate their behavior with us as her sister had been.

Gradually, Sabrina started to trust Tim and me. Her fear of her dishes, the back door, and the yard dissipated. She relaxed and started to develop a little confidence. During a reunion with Phoenix, she began to develop a spark of her own personality.

When Sabrina was reasonably confident with family life, we brought Kristine home. Sabrina and her sister recognized each other right away. They chased each other exuberantly and wrestled and tumbled around the yard. Kristine was still afraid of people and new sounds and objects, but she progressed quickly with her sister's help.

Unlike most herding dog parents, we were thrilled when the girls started nipping our calves. Of course, we taught them that this was a no-no, but their willingness to "cattle-dog" us demonstrated the strength of spirit that we had wanted so badly to see.

Our original plan had been to foster the pups until they were ready for their *fur*ever families, but we knew it would traumatize both us and the girls to send them off to a new home. So we accepted our status as "failed foster parents" and adopted them ourselves.

 *Charlotte Grider*

International Play Boy

I don't remember exactly when we first saw Quintana, but it was early on our Akumal, Mexico, vacation. He was a striking young Mexican lad with dark brown eyes. I remember his thin body jauntily trotting down the beach, ears and tail alert but unconcerned, as though he didn't have a care in the world. We made some sort of acknowledgement of each others' existence, and I remarked about how he could be our Border Collie's kid brother because they looked so much alike.

My son, Chris, coaxed him over, and soon they began to hang out together. The romance was on, and all of us were quickly drawn into the bonding process. We shared long walks on the beach together, day and night. I spent hours reading under a tree by our villa with him at my feet. We took home doggie bags from dinner to give to "our" doggie. (How often does that actually happen?) We were hooked!

I knew we had gone off the deep end when we began to get protective. On our walks across the highway, we would deliberately detour to try to lose him, lest he get too close to traffic. He would understand and patiently wait for our return at the last spot we were together. On another occasion, we curtailed our trip to the rocky point because he was obviously suffering from the heat of the rocks. Our Mexican friend returned in kind with equally bizarre behavior. He often swam out to where we were snorkeling, whining and pawing at us, literally begging us to get out of the water. When we obliged him by coming in, he danced around barking wildly, a joyous celebration of our safe return.

As our days in Akumal drew to a close, we all became concerned about the future of our friend. My husband suggested that we find his owner and offer a few bucks as a thank you for all the fun his dog had given us. I started asking around and got an answer I definitely didn't want to hear. The dog was indeed a stray, though he was being fed and cared for by the resort maintenance supervisor with the help of the hotel owners, some committed residents, and an occasional tourist donation. The man took care of all the beach dogs and saw to it that they received shots and medical attention when needed. He called "our" dog Quintana.

We planned to pitch in some money, of course, but I was still concerned for Quintana's plight. Then, as we sunned on the beach with Quintana at our sides on the day before we were scheduled to leave, I read an article in the local newsletter from a woman who had taken a beach dog back to Montana. She glowingly described her experience, but more importantly, she explained exactly how to bring a dog back to the U.S. It was easy. All we needed was some veterinary paperwork dated within 30 days of his departure. Additionally, the airline would charge a fee and require us to provide Quintana with a dog kennel.

I, of course, took this as a message from God. When I showed my husband the article, all he said was, "Shall we take him home?"

Chris and I immediately set off to make arrangements for our new pet, and the fates were with us. We ran into the maintenance man, who was delighted at the prospect of our adopting Quintana. He got us a vet appointment that afternoon, located a dog kennel and collar, and had me back out on the beach within a half hour. He also told us Quintana's history.

Quintana (meaning "gentle") had appeared there about a year and a half earlier, and had almost been adopted several times, but it never came to fruition. Thanks to the generosity of some dog lovers, he had been neutered, immunized, and treated for heartworm. The vet told us he had also survived a bout with distemper, as well as mange. After hearing all he had been through, I was even more convinced that our adoption was the right thing.

The trip home was almost anticlimactic. We breezed through customs in Miami and proceeded to Baltimore. Quintana was a trooper, and we arrived home to a chilly spring night in Maryland and a very jealous Border Collie.

Quintana's story has a happy ending, as he made the adjustment from stray to beloved pet very well. He assimilated easily into our pack. He put on weight, grew a long coat, and smiled when he greeted us. He preferred to be an indoor dog and was highly protective of his turf. He was our best-behaved dog. No shoes were chewed and no messes made. Quintana lived out his life peacefully with us until cancer took him at about age 12. He went peacefully in my arms, dying as a beloved pet.

Even with all its natural beauty, life is hard in the Yucatan, and many people are desperately poor. As in many emerging countries, dogs and cats are not a priority, and their lot is one of neglect, abuse, and starvation. We managed to remove one marvelous creature from this environment, but that's hardly a start. I would urge animal lovers who visit Mexico to support the rescue groups and the local humane society, Amigos de Mascotas, in their efforts to save these strays. Without your support, the care can't continue, and these animals will have no chance for a healthy life. Adopting a dog from Mexico is also a great choice, and the rewards are enormous.

 Pam Gardner

Summer Dreaming

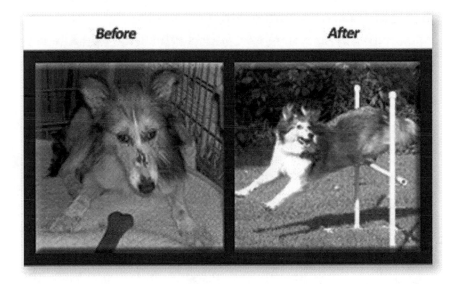

Imagine living in a filthy crate with only wire to support your feet. Imagine having litter after litter without veterinary care. Imagine suffering such bad skin issues that your entire body is covered in sores. If you can imagine these things, you can imagine the first three years of Summer's life in an Amish puppy mill. It could have been her *entire* life story if not for Lycoming County SPCA and, more specifically, a volunteer there named Summer, who rescued this mistreated pup along with several other dogs who were in terrible condition.

Summer was treated for all of her acute issues at the SPCA before finding her way into a Sheltie Rescue. Her life seemed to be taking a positive turn, but happiness wasn't meant for her... At least, not yet.

Though Summer still had many physical and emotional issues from her puppy mill days, she was adopted out to a kind woman and her husband. Trust was one of her greatest hurdles, which she was not able to overcome with her new dad. Back to the rescue she went. In foster care, she continued to struggle with trust, this time with the son of her foster mom. Summer was running out of options because the rescue had no other open foster homes, but instead of completely giving up on her, they passed her along to Northern Chesapeake Sheltie Rescue (NCSR) to see if she could find some help there.

Word went out through NCSR that a foster home was needed for this dear little dog. Even though I already had four Shelties in my home, I opened my door to this needy little girl, and she ended up staying for good.

Upon arrival, Summer still had many challenges to overcome. I searched for ways to help her with her severe allergies, dermatomyositis (aka "Sheltie skin syndrome"), and emotional issues. We sought veterinary care for her skin and agility instruction for her emotions, as the sport often aids dogs in gaining confidence.

Summer's skin quickly improved, and she loved agility so much that she even began to forget her fear of men when she was out on the field. Because she took to the sport so naturally, I took a chance and entered her in a trial. She was *brave*! Summer was beginning to blossom.

This sweet survivor continued her agility career for some time, earning her Novice and Open titles in AKC and her Agility Dog title in USDAA. She also earned some titles in CPE, another agility venue.

Summer's allergies have worsened as she has aged, which is typical, so these days we have refocused fun to indoor play with balls and toys in the house, away from the grass and pollen. Though Summer's beginnings were dark and gloomy, every day is now bright and sunshine-filled for her. Summer's title ribbons regularly remind me and those who visit that displaced, damaged dogs can thrive when you add a little love and a lot of confidence (and, of course, appropriate medical care).

 Marilyn Bradley

With Us in Spirit

We had a great bunch of dogs at our Texas home: Cirrus, our Samoyed, and Shadow and Mac, sister and brother blue merle Collies. Shadow's favorite place to go was Gaston's White River Resort in Bull Shoals, Arkansas. We took a trip to the Upper Peninsula of Michigan and stopped at Gaston's on the way there and back in July. We normally went in the fall, but at the time, we didn't know Shadow wouldn't be joining us there ever again.

She was diagnosed with ehrlichiosis, an auto-immune problem, after being bitten by a tick. The vet put her on medication and requested a follow-up at the end of August. On August 15th she would not eat. She had not previously shown any signs of being sick. I took her to the vet. She had a

103 fever. By the next day she was gone. Her body was trying to destroy the disease, and in the process had killed her. The veterinarians at Texas A&M said there was no hope to save her. She was only seven years, eight months, and 16 days old.

We were devastated. She was my little girl. And Mac was especially saddened because this was his little sister.

It's true what they say about one door closing and another opening, though. Our hearts broke for our loss, but my husband knew we had to move on. We had been looking at Houston Collie Rescue's website for a while, even before losing Shadow, and after her passing had seen a blue merle listed as a courtesy for a Great Pyrenees group out of Seguin, Texas. I told him it was too soon. He said it wasn't. This girl needed us as much as we needed her.

I contacted Val at the rescue, and she told me she was taking the dog, Spirit, to Dallas to meet another couple. I told her I would drive the four hours to meet her, too, if she would consider us. She agreed.

I took Cirrus and Mac with me because they would have to approve Spirit, too. As soon as they all met, they began to play. Spirit ran up to me, too, and I loved on her. It was like she knew I was going to be her new mom, and she was excited about it. She had come from a woman who had had 18 dogs, so I'm sure that sharing a home with only two others seemed just delightful. Both Val and I could see that she fit right in with us, so Val didn't hesitate to say she could be mine.

In the truck on the way home, Spirit sat in Shadow's favorite spot. Mac was not too sure about that, and for a while, he snapped at her every time she tried to lay her head on his back in the same way Shadow had. That all changed during our first trip out to Gaston's that October. In the car, Spirit again laid her head on his back, and this time Mac just looked at her and sighed. He had finally accepted her as his new little sister.

We all continue to miss Shadow, and we don't see Spirit as a replacement. We see her as a new chapter in our family book, a wonderful addition to our story, who has brought us out of our misery and elevated our spirits.

 *Linda Gandy*

Long Tails Short

Sato No Mo': Dandy was found roaming the streets of Puerto Rico by a group named Save-a-Sato ("sato" = street dog). There are over 100,000 "satos" roaming around Puerto Rico, and regrettably, rescues there usually don't end happily, with most dogs being abandoned again shortly after their adoption. Dandy's chances of finding a good home were slim, so a volunteer named La Lola contacted Houston Collie Rescue for help. Soon thereafter, Dandy found himself on a plane to his new foster home in Texas. Alice, his foster mom, was delighted to watch him grow more confident each day and felt sure he would make a wonderful companion for a lucky family. That family turned out to be right in Houston, where Dandy is now enjoying the good life he deserves. -*Pat Booher*

Transitions: Gill, a neglected Corgi, lived in a small rabbit hutch at a puppy mill for three years before he was rescued. When I adopted him, he was shy and scared of people. I brought him into a household with seven other dogs. In a year and a half, he has made a remarkable transition. He loves everyone now. He dances for his dinner and is one of the best dogs we have ever had. He has a doghouse in our den, which provides him some rabbit-hutch-like security when he needs it. He loves to chase us but does not bite our ankles like some Corgis are known to do. I am a Basset Hound lover, but because of Gill, Corgis have won my heart. -*Renee Kummerer*

The Dog Who Wouldn't Hunt

My husband, Dan, decided he wanted a Border Collie for herding sheep. It needed to be a black-faced one, which is rare for the breed. I wanted one of those classic Border Collies with a big, beautiful, white collar, white socks, and white tip on his tail. And I especially wanted one who would compete with me in agility.

As the president of Blue Ridge Border Collie Rescue, I keep an eye on Petfinder.com to find shelter dogs who may be better served by our rescue. One day I saw Shep, and he seemed to fit what my husband wanted, so I immediately asked Dan what he thought. He replied, "Let's get him. If he doesn't work out as a sheepdog, we'll foster him until we find him a home."

Shep had been turned in to a shelter in West Virginia because he "wouldn't hunt." This struck me as strange, since Border Collies aren't bred for hunting.

After getting Shep home and settled in, Dan decided to name him Bart. "Like Bart Simpson?" I asked.

"Yep!"

So Bart it was.

Since we didn't have our own sheep, Dan took Bart to a friend's farm. Dan came back saying, "He grabbed a sheep by the throat and took it down. He has too much prey drive to be a sheep dog." Maybe he was better suited for hunting?

Now what would I do with this dog? He had no manners and jumped in the air snapping his jaws if he thought I was going to throw a stick. He barked, pulled on the leash, chased cars, killed cats, peed in the house, ripped apart toys, nipped other dogs, and, in general, did not care much about what people had to say about him. What an obnoxious dog! Who would ever adopt him?

I had no intention of keeping Bart, but I thought that if I taught him some manners, he'd have a better chance of getting adopted. Additionally, I knew agility work would help bleed off some of his energy. To my surprise, Bart turned on to agility like a car chase onto a highway. He went crazy when he heard me playing with another dog, jumping our five-foot fence and darting through an agility tunnel to get to us. That was a shock! The more I worked him, the better and faster he got. If I gave him a bad command or didn't get my command out fast enough, Bart would bite me. I got bit a lot at first, which would make me shake my head and again think, "How will I ever get this dog adopted?"

Soon Bart stopped playing with other dogs and wouldn't leave my side. He had decided that I was his new mom. He knew he was staying before I did.

Even though Bart loved learning new things when we practiced agility, he was not the easiest dog to train. He bit his tongue every single time I worked with him. Most of our training sessions ended either with blood from Bart biting me or blood from Bart biting his tongue. (It turns out that his tongue *is* too big for his mouth.)

Though Bart was too skinny when he first came to our house, he didn't want to eat. He had a strange habit of spinning in his crate in my van if a car went by, if I drove backward, or if I went too fast around a turn. Short on time one morning, I put a bowl of dog food in the van crate, and instead of spinning when I backed up, Bart inhaled the food. This became our new ritual, and Bart finally started gaining weight.

Back to Bart's beginnings. I didn't know where he came from, but on the shelter's paperwork was an address. All I wanted to know was if Bart was a pure Border Collie, so I wrote to the address and included a self-addressed, stamped envelope plus an index card that said, "Is Shep a pure Border Collie? Circle yes or no."

I was trying to make it as easy as possible for someone to respond to me, but no one did. I waited and waited, but all I found out was that the address went to a business called Mail Boxes Etc. I was bummed.

One day several months later I received a phone call. A lady in Pennsylvania said she used to own my dog Seth. I was confused; my son's name was Seth. I had no idea which dog she was referring to since I rescue lots of dogs. Puzzled, I turned to Bart and said, "Seth."

He perked up and gave me a hug. Mystery solved. It turns out they had bought him for their eight-year-old boy for his birthday. He had an accident in the house, so they booted him outside to live in a kennel. He jumped out of the run, so they put him on a chain. He barked and barked. The neighbors complained. Seth had to go.

Instead of animal control taking him, Seth wound up on an organic farm to chase away deer. He not only chased deer but also cars, tractors, motorcycles, and anything else that moved. They tried a shock collar, but that didn't work, so they turned him over to a hunter in West Virginia, who renamed him Shep. I guess the guy figured he would use a Border Collie to hunt deer? Well, Shep is very afraid of gunshots, so he must have bolted at the first shot he heard. I have no doubt he was actually turned in to the shelter because of that fear, not because he wouldn't hunt.

Considering his background, it's amazing that Seth, who had been bounced around from home to inappropriate home, has now become Bart, the agility star for which I was originally searching. Last year Bart and I went to AKC Nationals. He was first in state and fourth in the nation for his jump division.

Bart has turned out to be my once-in-a-lifetime dream dog. He sleeps in our king-sized bed every night and goes with me everywhere. Words could never describe my feelings of love and pride for this dog. I always enjoy hearing "happy tales" from people who adopt dogs from me, and now I'm glad to be able to share my own.

 *Sylvia King*

Persistence Pays Off

© Vicki King

All through college I waited to get a dog of my own. I knew exactly what I wanted: a crazy, high drive, over-the-top Border Collie or Australian Shepherd for agility. Once I graduated and got my first job, I began looking on Petfinder.com for a one- or two-year-old Aussie or Border Collie. I noticed Willow and her piercing coyote-ish stare. She was perfect: petite, smooth-coated, and nearly solid white. Not only was she a beautiful dog, but her personality seemed to be just what I had been looking for. Her biography stated that she required a "special and understanding" home. She was less than a year old and had already been in two other homes.

I emailed the Pulaski County Animal Shelter in Virginia for more information. The news they sent back was unfortunate for me: She had been adopted by a young shelter volunteer and local college student. I was sad to have lost my chance to adopt her, but I continued looking and ended up adopting another dog, Odette, whom I was told was an Australian Shepherd-mix, but she turned out to be a Catahoula Leopard Dog.

I spent the next six months happily training my Catahoula, Odette. Although Catahoulas are officially "herding dogs" according to the AKC, many people are petitioning the organization to reclassify them as hunting dogs. I quickly found out why. They train like hounds! Odette clearly didn't have the herding instinct. Her stubborn streak, independence, and desire to always be the class clown kept me on my toes, but I still wished for a Border Collie or Australian Shepherd with the drive necessary for agility. I went back to Petfinder. com "just to look," and sure enough, there was Willow *again*!

Her bio was quite lengthy now. Her requirements were specific: She needed a family with a significant amount of herding-dog training experience, as this would be her last chance. The young college student who had adopted her did not understand a Border Collie's need to work. The student had left Willow tied up in the yard, so Willow chewed through her chain (three times) and ended up in biting situations. Finally, the student relinquished her back to animal control. Luckily, she won the heart of the animal control officer (who was also herding-dog experienced), and she was given one more try at finding a suitable home.

I called the shelter right away and faxed over my application. I spoke with the animal control officer and told her what I was looking for in a Border Collie. What most people tended to see as serious issues, I saw as great working-dog potential. Willow seemed to have every quality I needed; she was just lost and frustrated from never having a job to do. She was high energy, obsessive, and reactive.

I drove three hours that weekend to the shelter to meet her. I immediately noticed that her nervous energy manifested as frustration, as she would try to "get" any person or dog who walked near her. Most people would never consider a lunging dog, but I thought her energy was glorious! Obviously, it would take dedication to channel this dog's bad habits into positive outlets, but I saw how desperately she needed the type of working home I had to offer. If I didn't take her, she would be euthanized.

It has been five years since I brought home my frustrated and insecure 10-month-old Border Collie pup. She has blossomed into my dream come true. Now known as Henna, she trains and competes in AKC agility, obedience, and rally. She has earned so many titles that I can't even count them on my fingers. Henna is obsessed with her Frisbee and is a real natural at working livestock. She's versatile, able to run a lure course with the sight hounds and leap ocean waves with Retrievers. She will do anything I ask of her. Henna has finally found her purpose and her job. She is a dog who will always require a watchful eye and an experienced handler. She is very reactive to the environment and needs to be monitored closely around children, other dogs, and people who give her too much direct eye contact, but give her a job to do, and her focus is like a laser.

Henna is the poster dog for Border Collies that end up in homes with nothing to do. Since entering a home that is performance-oriented rather than pet-oriented, she has excelled at everything I have asked of her. She was given a second, well, *third* chance at having a good life, and she gave me a second chance at having a true working-breed dog.

Oh, you were wondering about Odette? She's doing fine! She just turned nine and still competes in agility, obedience, and rally on occasion. She and Henna are best friends/sisters. Both have taught me so much as far as training and showing are concerned. For example, while I use regular treats at the end of the weave poles to motivate Henna, Odette requires my spaghetti dinner, still in the glass bowl, offered from the end of my fork! The two are polar opposites; Henna lives to work, and Odette prefers to keep me laughing.

Both of these dogs are awesome. The two are quite a pair, having both overcome a lot in their past. They have "trained" me to be the handler I am today, and I would not have had the success I've had in the ring with other dogs if it were not for these two girls. My Border Collie makes me look like a very good handler, and my Catahoula keeps me grounded, humble, and always on my toes.

 Rachel Shaw

Foxy Lady

I met Foxy on a warm October day at Pet Fest in Old Town Spring, Texas. She had been seized from a hoarder by the Houston SPCA, which had then turned her over to Houston Collie Rescue for placement. It was absolutely love at first sight. She was a beautiful smooth Collie, the most petite I had ever seen. And she had spunk. Her little size did not faze her! She really made an impression on me. By the time Pet Fest was over, I knew we were going to take Foxy home as a foster.

At home everyone fell in love with her. We already had two other smooth Collies from that seizure, so it was like a family reunion for all three of them. We think Foxy and our Dakota must have been mother and son because of the way they nuzzled and played and romped; they slept together and were totally inseparable.

Within a month or so, there was an adoption request for Foxy. Our hearts were torn. She was our first "real" foster dog, and we struggled with the idea of sending her to a new home. She just seemed to fit in so well. Even so, we had a job to do.

The adopters traveled from west Texas to come pick her up. It took everything I had to let her go with them. As it turned out, I shouldn't have worried about never seeing Foxy again. The adoptive home turned out to be a bad match for her, so they graciously sent her back to be with us forever before choosing another Collie who was a much better fit for their budding family.

Foxy officially became ours right before Christmas. We were overjoyed to have her back. Her antics brought love and laughter into our home.

In May of the following year, I had a medical emergency. and Foxy stayed right by my side. She climbed up on my bed and laid her head in my lap, looking up at me reassuringly and patting my face with her paw. I truly felt like God had sent her to be there with me. She kept me grounded for an hour before help arrived. For that, I will always be grateful to her.

Two months later Foxy began to have intermittent digestive problems. I took her to the vet, but nothing seemed amiss, so he prescribed medicine to help balance out her system. She would seem fine for a while, and then her symptoms would return. We changed dog food and consulted with the vet several times, but her illness was elusive, baffling even the most seasoned of veterinarians.

In September of that year, a few days before Hurricane Ike hit Galveston Island, we were preparing for the approaching storm when Foxy fell ill again. I rushed her to the emergency vet, where she received IV fluids and had a radiograph of her stomach done. The vets suspected bloat, a common problem in herding dogs. We were so worried! The radiograph did not show bloating but did indicate a possible blockage in her intestines. The vets would have to perform exploratory surgery to truly determine what was going on.

Foxy was diagnosed with an intussusception, a condition where one portion of the intestine slides into the next, much like the pieces of a telescope. It completely explained the intermittent digestive issues. The vet told us it was probably genetic. Her chances for survival depended on whether or not the intestines re-collapsed, which can sometimes happen. They did in her case.

We lost Foxy in the midst of the hurricane, with the pounding wind and rain outside echoing the tears and heartbreak we all felt. I think Dakota mourned her loss the most.

The outpouring of well-wishes and sympathy from the members of Houston Collie Rescue was unbelievable. It made us feel like we were part of an exclusive "family."

We have a small, round plaque that the vet made for us of Foxy's paw print on our fireplace mantle. I pick it up from time to time, closing my eyes, running my hand across her imprint, and remember the delicate little kisses she used to give on my cheek. I reflect on the good times and what a joy and blessing she was to us, and I know that one day she will meet me at the Rainbow Bridge. In the meantime, I envision her running and playing, being her spunky self, with all of the other Collies in that beautiful place.

 *Tia Hurt*

Alec Bald-One

Alec and his cage partner, Billie, were so matted that the shelter they landed in was forced to shave them down. Thus, they became Alec and Billie Bald-One. (Shaving a Sheltie is *not* recommended: They have that coat for a reason. It insulates them by providing heat in winter and cool in summer. Without that coat, they can become wind-burned, sun-burned, or frost-bitten. This was a special circumstance.)

The duo could barely walk. Apparently they had spent their lives in a cage together, barely setting foot on the ground.

Because of their terrible condition, the shelter asked Central Ohio Sheltie Rescue (COSR) to rehabilitate them. Right from the start, the pair put their paw prints on everyone's hearts. Billie was quiet and shy; he curled up in a ball and did not want to be touched. Alec was more outgoing.

I volunteered for the rescue, and for weeks I waited for someone to adopt Alec. I could not believe that no one wanted to give him a forever home. Perhaps his lack of hair put some people off; he just did not look like a Sheltie to outsiders, but like many rescue volunteers, I saw him for what he could be and not for he was when he initially arrived. To me, Alec Bald-One was absolutely beautiful.

Finally, I could no longer stand by and watch this adorable little guy long for his forever home. I told the rescue that I would open my home to Alec, and I am so glad that I took that step. He fit right in with my other adopted Sheltie, Eddye, bonding as though they had always been friends. The two of them regularly frolicked and played together before settling down to enjoy my company, too. Alec turned out to be sweet, ornery, and 14.5 pounds of red-headed joy. Despite his legs being a little crooked from his previous life in a crate, he hasn't slowed down for a minute, not even in snow. His favorite thing is to catch snowballs, a game he learned from watching Eddye.

Though Eddye is now gone, I feel fortunate to have adopted these Shelties and made them a part of my life. Both have been spoiled rotten, but why have a dog if you're not going to spoil him a little? (Or, in my case, *a lot*.) They have given me so much in return. For example, whether I'm coming in from a long day at work or from a short walk to the mailbox, my dogs have given me a celebration. They happily greet me as though I have been away for months, which brings a smile to my heart and brightens my day.

Above all else, the dogs in my life have been my friends. I can tell that they know and appreciate the fact that they have been rescued. Some people want puppies. Puppies are great, but I'll take a calmer, more mature dog any day. Thank goodness for rescues like COSR that help to connect people with these wonderful furry friends.

 *Renee Engelbach*

Note: *Billy Bald-One was adopted and is also thriving.*

Blue-Eyed Belle

Annabelle came into our lives after we already had a pack of dogs from shelters, rescues, and less-than-perfect circumstances: Linus, our loving Border Collie; Charlie, our bossy Australian Shepherd; Jake, our big baby Australian Shepherd; Riley, our silly Lhaso Apso; and Chloe, our "mother hen" black Labrador Retriever. You could say that our house was pretty dog friendly.

When our 12-year-old Chloe started having health and mobility problems, my husband and I began discuss adding another female to our pack. When Chloe passed, we would all miss her dearly, and our pack would be without its mama. We knew we'd need another girl to keep all the boys in line.

My husband and I love Border Collies for their sweetness, intelligence, sensitivity, loyalty, and loving nature. Our Linus was a perfect example of the breed – a dream dog – so the new girl would have to be a Border Collie, too.

We had already heard about Nebraska Border Collie Rescue when we went to the Horse Expo in Lincoln. After talking with some rescue volunteers, we were convinced that when we were ready to adopt, it would be from them. I checked their website regularly, often feeling tempted to inquire about one or two dogs, but something kept getting in the way. That is, until a cold November day, when I saw our beautiful, blue-eyed Annabelle. I know it sounds crazy, but one look at her sweet face, and I knew she was the girl for our family.

Needless to say, I filled out the adoption application that day. I remember how nervous my husband and I were. We knew we were responsible with our pets, but we didn't know if they would recognize that in us.

Annabelle's foster parents contacted us a few days later to set up a meeting. When the pickup truck drove down our driveway and Annabelle jumped out, my husband and I were instantly in love. She was a gigantic pile of hairy, black-and-white love with two shiny, beautiful, blue eyes.

As our dogs crazily sniffed, jumped, ran, barked, licked, and showed off their toys, Annabelle maintained her composure, simply taking in all the new sights, smells, and sounds. After meeting her soon-to-be brothers and sister, she romped through the house and yard. She seemed pleased. When the visit was over, we were sad to see her go but hopeful that she would be back soon for good.

The next day we got the call. Annabelle would join our family permanently. Overjoyed, the following week we picked her up and made it official with a new, hot pink, zebra-striped collar. Later that night, when all the dogs were exhausted from the excitement of bringing Annabelle home to live with us, Annabelle crawled up on my lap – all 66 pounds of her – and rested her head on my neck and shoulder. She gave me a full and total body hug, remaining that way for an entire hour. It was as if she was asking me to please keep her, telling us she wanted to stay. I remember looking across the room at my husband with teary eyes and telling him that she knew she was finally in her forever home.

Our house has been a love-fest ever since that cold November night. Annabelle has two boyfriends, as Linus and Jake are both smitten with her. She is totally obsessed with toys, taking each one out of the toy box to show me every night. She loves going on long walks, running after the horses, managing the boys, and following around the cats, Tinkerbell and Kiki. She has also become my constant shadow.

The other amazing part of this story is that Chloe is still with us. Annabelle's arrival helped Chloe find a new purpose in life, and showing her the ropes has kept Chloe active and alert.

To this day, I often look into Annabelle's kind, stunning eyes and wonder about her life before she came to our house. I wish she could tell me her whole story. Was her tummy always full? Did she have a soft place to rest her head? Did she ever have a family that loved her? Her story may not have had a great beginning, but it will definitely have a very happy ending.

 *Tracey Wieser*

Long Tails Short

Carpenter Collie: When I first adopted my nine-month-old Collie, Wyatt, I kept him crated when I was out because he tended to get into trouble when left alone. When he was 18 months old, and after leaving him uncrated for short trips to the store, I decided he was ready to stay out for extended periods of time. That is, until he shredded my new coffee table. There was literally a pile of sawdust on the floor that was so high it clogged my vacuum. Needless to say, he went back in the crate when I was not home. When he was two, I tried again to leave him out. This time I came home to an antique doll with the legs chewed off. It cost me $500 to have her repaired. I took him to the Blessing of the Animals at a local church after the second event, hoping he would see the light, but instead, I did. I love my Collie and would not trade him for anything, but he is back in his crate until further notice. -*Linda Chesser*

Sheltie Hands: It turns out Shelties believe that their front paws are, in fact, hands. Every one of my Shelties has, on any number of occasions, attempted to catch with his front paws, and generally, each has been successful! They also hold their chew treat with their front paws in a peculiar way at times. Second Chance takes this to an extreme. He actually looks very squirrel-like when he tries to catch tennis balls with his "hands." He also like to "hold hands" with humans.-*Renee Engelbach*

Runs with Diapers

When puppy Jasmine got a urinary infection, it seemed like all I did was clean up dribbles of urine. The fact that she had been pretty close to housetrained flew right out the window. That is, until I found a pair of little denim doggie pants that I had packed away in my dog supply box. (I just knew I would have another need for them one day.)

Seeing that I would be in trouble once my puppy wet the only pair of pants I had for her, my co-worker sent me home with a package of disposable doggie diapers in pretty patterns of pink checkers and polka dots. Who knew there even was such a thing?

Anyone who has tried to put a diaper on a wiggly toddler single-handedly has had an easier job than I! Picture one excited puppy racing in from the back yard, ready to run and wrestle with the other dogs; meanwhile one lone, hopeful person stands between her and total bliss, poised for the catch with one hand, while the other shakes open a diaper. I catch her easily enough, but I quickly realize that I need many more than two hands to accomplish said task. Thinking that my hands and legs can work together to stabilize Jasmine and manipulate the diaper, I try to hold her still between my legs with my calves. My free hand makes several attempts to poke her wagging tail through the small hole in the back of the diaper, but by the time I'm successful, Jazzy has managed to contort herself and now lies upside-down between my feet. Her tail is back out of the diaper, wagging wildly while she tries to escape. What a grand new game I have invented for her!

I lift her up into a standing position once again and reposition her between my legs with her head facing behind me. This gives me a clear view and easy(ish) access to her tail. Whether it's because she is deaf and can't hear me or because she can't see exactly what my hands are doing to her rear end (or perhaps because she *can* see what I'm up to), we repeat the wiggling scenario several times before I get it right. As Jazzy continues to wiggle and leap between my legs, I consider that I really need to start working on my leg muscles!

Tails make great handles, and when I finally get the tail through the tail hole for the third time, I grab it to prevent it from wiggling back out. My other hand now pulls the rest of the diaper down to her belly between her rear legs. Now what? My hands are both busy, as are my legs. Jazzy is still wiggly, although not so much as before. She's now entertaining herself by grabbing and shaking the back of my pant legs with her teeth.

By removing my hand from her tail and sliding it to hold the upper part of the diaper on her back, I now have one hand on the top and one on the bottom... And the tail is still in the tail hole! The other dogs are all gathered around, curious about this new game Jazzy seems to be enjoying, and I have no free hands to shoo away their curious noses.

I'm finally able to maneuver my hands to attach the diaper flaps, one side and then the other. I make one final, last-minute adjustment to even it up before releasing the bucking bronco from my grasp. I breathe a deep sigh of relief, proud of my success.

Though Jasmine didn't take to the idea at first – somehow managing to run in a straight line across the floor while spinning and reaching for the diaper with her teeth – I'm happy to report that the diaper application became easier each time, with Jasmine becoming, dare I say, *cooperative*! Even so, I'm happy that she only had to wear them for a couple days until the medications kicked in and the peeing stopped. I don't recall diapering being an Olympic sport, but after my experience with Jasmine, I would say it should be!

 Debbie Bauer

For Friends and Furry Family

I've had the opportunity to love four different Australian Cattle Dogs (ACDs). My first was a mix. His father was a full-blooded ACD, and his mother was a full-blooded Boston Terrier. Buddy turned out beautiful: almost every characteristic was ACD, but he was smaller – around 30 pounds – and he had slender legs and small feet like his mother. For me, he was the *perfect* dog. He cuddled if I wanted to cuddle, played if I wanted to play. He was extremely well-behaved and intelligent. He loved me with all his heart and completely ignored, to the point of being rude, everyone else. Buddy was my baby for 11 years before he finally succumbed to lymphoma.

I waited two years before I getting another dog. Along came Nikko: he was six weeks old, and little did I know, he had distemper (a fatal but easily preventable viral disease). It was touch-and-go for a few days before he pulled through. Nikko was my problem child; he pushed the envelope every single day (actually many times a day). I thought I was a bad mother until a veterinarian finally told me that Nikko had neurological damage from the distemper. That eased my guilt a bit, but just imagine what life is like with a full-blood ACD with brain damage! I used to tell people that the Lord was testing me with Nikko and I failed, which is why He would not give me children.

Nevertheless, I loved Nikko with all my heart. I was heartbroken when I lost him to cancer after nine years together. I didn't even want to go home in the evenings because Nikko wasn't there, and my significant other, Jay, usually worked late.

I only made it a week and a half without a dog following Nikko's passing. I was miserable. I looked at ACD websites regularly, even though everything I had read said not to look too soon, especially not for another dog who looks like the one you had before. One day I saw five full-blood ACDs in the Cartersville, Georgia, pound. Their time to find homes was limited. I contacted Melissa Tooley at Carolina ACD Rescue & Rebound (R&R) and told her I would foster two if she pulled them from the shelter. In my head I was thinking, "*What* am I doing?" but I didn't let those thoughts stop me. I just kept telling myself that it was only fostering – no commitments. I was concerned that getting a dog so soon would be dishonorable to Nikko, but fostering would be fine, right?

R&R pulled Doc and Dinah from the shelter three days before they were to be put down. Doc was about three years old and had been abused. Dinah was about 11 months old and had been neglected. Doc was skittish because of his apparent mistreatment, but after six months of me loving on him, he finally started loving on me back. Dinah got past her fears rather quickly and turned out to be a cutie-pie who loved to play.

I finally adopted Doc and Dinah a few months after taking them in. I delayed telling Jay for about a week for fear he would be upset, but when I finally did, he said, "I knew you were going to adopt them the day we brought them home."

Things rocked along smoothly for several months; Doc and Dinah were both a dream! Then a string of tough breaks occurred. Jay and I separated after eight years together; I encountered some rather severe financial issues; and my car was totaled (the other person's fault). The car was old, and the insurance company didn't give me much for it, but I managed to get a vehicle quickly enough to make the two-week trip I had planned to visit my brother's home for Christmas. I had not been home for three years, so, of course, I didn't want to miss this, especially not with the opportunity to make family introductions with Doc and Dinah for the first time. Then I had a heart attack over Christmas.

Amidst all these unfortunate events, I couldn't help but entertain the idea of taking my own life. But each time that thought crossed my mind, I immediately had to consider what would happen to Doc and Dinah. Who would care for them? Family wasn't an option. During this time, sweet Melissa from the rescue became my rock. She emailed encouragement, called to check on me and the pups, and showed sincere concern and caring.

That's when it hit me that the Lord had a plan for me, even back when I first made the call to offer to foster Doc and Dinah months earlier. Then I knew for sure that I had not dishonored Nikko's memory. He couldn't hang on to help me through, so he sent me two babies who could.

The closeness between my dogs and me grows stronger every day. I have the best of both worlds in this pair. Doc is my love-bug who would *cuddle* all the time. Dinah is my spitfire who would *play* all the time.

As for me, I'm doing much better. Between cardiac rehab, dietary monitoring, support from my friends, and love from my dogs, I am very much on my way to recovery. I feel blessed to have been associated with R&R and Melissa, and I am especially thankful for my two fur babies, Doc and Dinah. They saved my life after I saved theirs!

 *Connie Jackson*

Once a Herder

Years ago I met my fiancé, Jack, when I was adopting my first Border Collie. Since then we have fostered a number of Border Collies for Nebraska Border Collie Rescue and have seen them go to very happy homes. One foster dog, Dalyel, was surrendered to the rescue group because the owner competed in herding trials and felt that Dalyel just wasn't up to snuff.

Jack and I took Dalyel into our home. Instantly, she latched onto me and became my little shadow. We noticed that loud noises would send her hiding, and any command or correction would produce the same effect, no matter how soft our voices. Our assessment of Dalyel was that she was one scared pup and was not ready to be adopted until we could figure out how to work her through her issues. We took her out to play fetch one day with the other dogs, and Dalyel's herding instincts came rushing back to the surface. She targeted my big, white Border Collie who could be compared to a lamb and tried to herd him.

Jack and I decided to take her to our good friend John Holman, a national herding champion, to see what he thought about Dalyel's herding instincts. He put her in a round pen with a few sheep and observed her. She instantly showed interest, but 30 seconds later she ran over to the fence where Jack and I stood and tried to claw her way out. It was heartbreaking to see her so interested in the sheep and then so completely terrified. John came back and said that because of her interest in the sheep, he wanted to continue working with her. He told us that he would not put any pressure on her; he would work with her at her pace. Because of her aversion to correction, he was going to try to school her back through the herding basics without using any voice commands or hand signals.

During the second lesson, the sheep held Dalyel's interest for a full minute before she came over and sat by the fence where I was standing. John asked me to join him in the pen to help encourage her. I had never had a herding lesson before, but John was right there showing me what to do. Then Dalyel started following the sheep! We gave her a ton of praise and ended on a good note.

Since then, Dalyel and I have had many lessons with John, and she and I have bonded and become inseparable. We thought it would be fun to compete in an AKC herding trial. Not only was it a blast, but we won our very first herding certificate! Almost a year after Dalyel came into rescue, Jack and I decided to adopt her into our family. She has really come out of her shell and is happiest when she's out at John's farm working his sheep.

Her previous owner did such a wonderful thing by surrendering Dalyel to the rescue group. If it hadn't been for him, I never would have found my little co-pilot and herding partner.

 *Audrey Campbell*

The "Untrainable" Champion

© Furry Fotography

I really wanted a teammate for the high-speed dog sport of agility, so I turned to Blue Ridge Border Collie Rescue (BRBCR) to help me find one. My previous rescue dog's foster mom, Sylvia, helped me by searching the Eastern Seaboard for the right fit, looking into all types of rescues and shelters. After months of searching, she found Cooper.

Cooper had been living in an outdoor crate throughout the Virginia winter because his owner had deemed him "untrainable" at six months of age. Anne, a neighbor, spotted this abuse and bought the dog with good intentions, but she had no idea what to do once baby Border Collie boredom set in and Cooper started "entertaining" himself. Anne contacted BRBCR for help, which is when Sylvia first heard about Cooper. She thought he seemed perfect for me, so she connected me with Anne.

I was so excited that we might have found the dog of my dreams, until I found out that Anne really liked Cooper, too. After several hours on the phone, she had cold feet about giving him up. I was deflated: so close, yet so far. I told her to take some time and think it over, and the next day I received a tear-filled call from her saying that she just wanted to do right by Cooper, and right meant sending him to me!

I was elated but also apprehensive that Anne might change her mind, since she was so emotionally invested in this dog. I called Sylvia, and miraculously, she arranged for her son's ultimate Frisbee team to pick Cooper up from Anne at an exit off the highway. Success! Cooper arrived at Sylvia's house (also in Virginia) to be fostered until I could drive up from Florida to get him.

Six years later Cooper is an amazing and resilient dog, despite having been shuffled around from home to home to home as a puppy. He has been both a blast and a challenge, to be sure. As a super high-drive Border Collie who just wants to work, Cooper excels at agility and also takes his unofficial jobs as Frisbee-catcher, pond-swimmer, and stick-mover very seriously. He is a ham who thrives on lively crowds, wowing them with antics like death-defying leaps off obstacles or occasionally over a human; running amuck; and performing complex sequences in, on, and around agility equipment. He has achieved multiple agility championships in four venues (AKC, CPE, NADAC, and USDAA), and he has earned more than 100 titles to date. Not bad for an "untrainable" dog.

Surprisingly, Cooper has turned out to be extremely confident and composed. At one trial, he was in the ring when a large dog got loose from his handler and charged him, hackles raised and lips snarled. Cooper just stopped running and looked at the dog as if to say, "You might want to rethink this."

When the dog wilted under Cooper's stern gaze and immediately returned to his owner, Cooper simply returned to his job of performing a qualifying run. I was simply a bystander; Cooper had it handled with grace and confidence.

Cooper continues to run agility and works as my "school" dog, teaching other handlers about finesse and patience. Cooper's brand of agility is all about pressure and space, patience, and balance. It is about holding on for the run and waiting for the opportunity. In a way, Cooper's approach to agility is reminiscent of his puppyhood: patiently waiting to excel and exceed expectations.

I can never thank BRBCR and Sylvia enough for going that extra mile to find and foster Cooper. I'm also grateful to Anne, who not only had the heart to take him in but also the courage to trust in me to care for him. She still keeps in touch, and she has since rescued several more dogs and placed them in forever homes. I would like to think that Cooper inspired her, but some people are just destined to save souls. Rescuers, fosters, and volunteers are really the unsung heroes for some amazing dogs. They give dogs like Cooper a chance at a forever home and people like me an opportunity to find a life-changing friend.

 Gill Chapman

Most Improved Team

THE AMAZING DEAF CATTLE DOG PROMOTES CHARACTER IN YOUNG STUDENTS

Special to the Reporter-Herald

I brought Angelyne into my life when she was eight weeks old. I was smitten by how she tapped my knee with her nose when we met three weeks earlier, as if to say, "I'm picking you." She was the one I wanted. Her greeting, combined with her unique mannerisms and beautiful color, struck me as exceptional. At the time, I had no idea that she had been born bi-laterally deaf.

Angelyne was 12 weeks old when we started puppy obedience class. In addition to her being my companion, I was considering a future with her in agility or flyball. During the second week of class, our teacher, Laura Bevacqua, told me she believed Angelyne was deaf and recommended Dr. Robin Downing from the Windsor Veterinary Clinic in Windsor, Colorado, for Angelyne's hearing test, examination, and further advice.

At our appointment, Downing explained that genetics and breeding imperfections cause deafness in Australian Cattle Dogs (ACDs) and other breeds. Upon Downing's diagnosis of Angelyne's deafness, I questioned my future with and without her. I had fallen in love with her, but I assumed failure was imminent. I knew that it would not be right to just give her up, as I had heard about how often deaf dogs were abused and/or euthanized, but would I really be able to raise and train a deaf dog?

I doubted whether I could give Angelyne a normal and fulfilling life. I considered quitting obedience class, yet we returned. I realized that keeping Angelyne would be a labor of love and commitment with no guarantee of success, but the positives outweighed the doubts and fear. I was in love with Angelyne. I had a working knowledge of ACDs and the support of people like Downing and Bevacqua. Our success would take much time, patience, compassion, and belief that accomplishment could come from uncertainty. One attribute that I knew could benefit my outlook with Angelyne was the resilience I developed growing up with and facing my lifelong challenge with type 1 diabetes.

In the end, that puppy obedience class not only gave us a solid base of training but helped us create the bond and mission we are known for today. Angelyne and I were awarded "Most Improved Team" in class. We graduated with a new confidence that we could persevere, despite my fears. I created most of our hand signals and body language commands. Bevacqua showed us a few of our first signals but most of our signals are non-ASL (American Sign Language) and were born by thinking outside of the box.

By the time Angelyne was a year and a half old, we had created and mastered 22 different hand signals and commands. I was amazed by how much we accomplished in such a short time. From the start of our training, we noticed many people gathering around to watch. Most people had no idea Angelyne was deaf until I told them. Angelyne's uncanny ability to connect with people of all ages, abilities, and social situations quickly became apparent.

An astute neighbor, who was convinced that Angelyne was the most awesome dog he had ever seen, convinced us to enter a local dog talent show. We competed against 10 other dogs and won. After the show, a local newspaper reporter interviewed us for an online news video and several people approached us with invitations to bring our story and performance to them. Since that first public appearance many years ago, we've won 11 dog talent shows and made more than 240 presentations.

In 2009, I dedicated my life to promoting Angelyne, "The Amazing DEAF Cattle Dog," as an inspiration to people throughout the Rocky Mountain region. Our mission is now multi-faceted, with character education programs for schools, motivational and inspiring speeches and poems, a deaf dog training program, and our eye-catching trick demonstration using our 40+ hand signals and body language commands. Additionally, we never pass up an opportunity to promote adoption, especially that of deaf dogs and the Australian Cattle Dog breed.

Sometimes the best things in life happen when you're not expecting them. Angelyne is the best thing that has happened to me, forever changing who I am and who I want to be. Though at first, I wasn't sure how having a deaf dog would affect my life and whether I could care for her, it is *because* of Angelyne's deafness that I have learned to be a teacher, inspirer, leader, companion, provider, buddy, and best friend.

What seemed at first to be an insurmountable challenge was, in fact, an unexpected blessing.

 Eric Melvin

Farr Regional Library:
Best wishes always!
Eric & Angelyne
The Amazing DEAF Cattle Dog

Angelyne
The Amazing DEAF Cattle Dog

Long Tails Short

Peaceful Pooch: Bandit was a skinny, one-year-old, deaf pup with missing teeth, a collapsed trachea, and torn anterior cruciate ligaments (ACLs) in both legs. He was unique among the dogs on the rescue website because of his overwhelming issues. As I filled out the adoption application, I had some of the other dogs in mind, but I found myself typing "Bandit" instead. His foster mom called and told me that he was a fireball, and since I had experience with deaf Cattle Dogs, she thought we might be a good match. She was right! In my experience, deaf Cattle Dogs are so sensitive and smart that you hardly know they are deaf. They just have a different ability. Like my previous deaf dog, Jenta, Bandit is learning to respond to flashlight signals at night. It's peaceful and quiet – no yelling – and I only need to take special care with traffic and people who might mistakenly startle him. Bandit's legs have been repaired, and we are working on obedience. I'm looking forward to another awesome journey together with my rockin' deaf dog. -*Mimi Brown*

Therapy From the Soul: Spirit's Amazing Grace, whom I adopted five years ago from Houston Collie Rescue, is beautiful both on the outside and on the inside. She is everyone's favorite in the nursing homes and elementary schools we visit for pet therapy and humane education. People can tell how happy she is to be there by her prancing gait. At times Spirit gets surrounded by more than 30 children, which she thinks is the greatest thing in the world. Spirit makes Houston Collie Rescue proud! –*Susan Papa*

Unpredictable

It was a typical spring day at the Downtown Dog and Cat, a doggie daycare in Denver, Colorado, where New Hope Cattle Dog Rescue & Rehoming was hosting an adoption event. I had become a foster home provider for the organization a month earlier and was at the event with my first foster dog, a stunning Husky/Blue Heeler mix named Shiloh.

A young couple had taken a liking to Shiloh, and she would be going home with them. Though I had housed Shiloh for only a month, a feeling of melancholy crept over me as I realized I might never see her again. Her cute leap as she bounded along in the park, the way she stayed by my side, her gorgeous face, all those things would soon belong to someone else.

So what's the remedy for this kind of sadness? "It's time to get another foster dog," one of the long-time foster parents suggested.

That seemed logical enough to me. Shiloh now had her forever home, so I had an open spot in my house for another dog waiting to find a family. Though my husband, Andres, and I already had two cats and a Red Heeler of our own, I had somehow convinced him that there was just enough room in our household for another temporary, otherwise homeless resident. We were already walking, feeding, and cleaning up after Moby, so what's one more?

As Shiloh's adoption papers were signed, I began to wonder who my next foster dog would be. One of the organizers said I would be taking home Pepper, a calm, easygoing, older, petite Blue Heeler girl whose face resembled a fox. She had not yet been adopted, and since the event was nearing its end, she would soon need a place to go. I imagined the interaction between Pepper and Moby, and I envisioned a quaint friendship like the one that had developed between him and Shiloh. Done and done. Pepper would be perfect. Plus, Andres would be happy to have a dog who was older and not quite so energetic.

I had been watching Pepper when a volunteer approached and asked if I would be open to taking home a different dog. "Dixon is very shy, and the plan is to have him stay in dog daycare to get socialized," she said.

After a pause, she added, "But... I really don't know if that's going to be best for him. If he is with a family, he'll have more opportunities to build his confidence and learn how to be with people."

She looked towards Dixon, a black-and-white speckled dog with patches of black, ears that looked like folded-over triangles, and eyes that resembled a Rottweiler's. His tail was between his legs, and he ran away from anyone who came within four feet of him. The foster coordinator needed to get a number off of his collar, which entailed getting close enough to him to remove his tags. He wouldn't come to anyone, even for food, and eventually eight volunteers had to create a "human wall" to keep him from darting away.

"That dog over sweet Pepper?" I thought. "He's going to be hard to love. No way is he coming home with me!"

Fortunately, my pessimistic thoughts didn't translate to words, and instead I said, "Well, okay."

After all, I had become a foster parent because I wanted to help dogs, and this was one who especially needed some care. I heard that some workers from the shelter that he had come from had been less than optimistic about his ability to fit into a family. His papers described him as "very scared," and he certainly wasn't enthusiastic about having his ears massaged or belly rubbed like the other dogs.

In my car he stayed in the back seat, keeping a wary eye on me as I started to drive. The stress of the adoption event soon became apparent as he drifted off to sleep while the car hummed along. His chest went up and down rapidly, and I could hear him breathing out of his nose as he rested. It was a serene moment in what must have been a very chaotic day for him.

We soon arrived at my husband's parents' house, where Andres was waiting for me. I told him that Shiloh had been adopted and then sheepishly said that I had gotten another foster dog.

"You got another one?" he exclaimed, a little annoyed.

I told him that it would just be for a little while, and this dog could really use some help. "Okay," he murmured hesitantly as he came out to see the new dog.

Dixon peered at us with trepidation as I led him to the back yard where Moby was waiting. We left the dogs together, so they could sniff each other and perform the other formalities of dog acquainting.

Later, when I went outside to get something from the car, a neighbor asked, "Is that your dog?" Confused, I turned around, and there, in the middle of the street, was Dixon. He must have jumped the fence!

"Dixon, come here!" I said in the calmest voice I could muster.

He regarded me with caution before turning to run the opposite way. "No, come back!" I yelled.

He continued to run, crossing a busy street in the process. I took off after him, sprinting as fast as I could. Unless you're an Olympic athlete, keeping up with a dog is a difficult task. I thought I was lucky when I cornered him in a yard, but he deftly escaped and was soon out of my sight again.

I rushed back to the house, tears flowing uncontrollably. With four busy streets within a half-mile radius, I could only imagine the dangerous possibilities. My husband met me with the car, and we combed the neighborhood. No sign of Dixon; I was inconsolable. Soon realizing the futility of our search, we returned to the house. As I walked up to the front door, I checked the back yard, holding out an ounce of hope that Dixon might have returned. Lo and behold, he was there! Though he was still scrutinizing me and keeping his distance, he was safe. We figured that he came back for his new friend, Moby, who had stayed in the back yard the whole time.

During the next two weeks, something surprising happened. The dog who had seemed unlovable, shy, scared, and disinterested in human contact proved to be anything but. One night, while I sat on the floor, he came up unexpectedly and wanted to be caressed in my lap. This, from the little dog who previously had not allowed anyone near him!

From that moment on, Dixon has been our dog, giving and receiving a pure kind of love that is a testimony to the power of human and animal bonds. We renamed him Diggs, as he has a penchant for digging, but now he faithfully comes to both of us when we call out his name. We were always his forever home, although we never could have predicted it!

 Karin Alvarez

Comfort

Acouple weeks before Thanksgiving, Houston Collie Rescue was notified of a senior female Collie in a shelter in San Antonio, Texas. Thanks to a wonderful group of volunteers, we were able to transport the lovely girl to Spring, Texas. When I saw her sweet face in the shelter photo, I knew I was meant to foster her.

I had just lost my senior Collie, Bella, in July, and my best friend and roommate agreed that we should foster her. Willow, as we named her, was between 12 and 14 years old. Because she was covered in feces and urine, she had to be shaved.

Upon meeting her, I could not imagine how anyone could have lost her and not been frantically searching for her. In Texas, to receive a senior dog who is not heartworm positive is rare, so at some point someone must have been giving her heartworm preventative.

Willow was sweet, intelligent, and funny. She learned how to open the screen door to follow me inside. To me, this was more proof that she couldn't have gotten lost on her own; she was too devoted and loyal to her humans.

In January I decided to adopt her. It was important to me that when her time came she had a family of her own, not just a foster family.

In April three of my Collies and my roommate Ellie's Collie, Ceanna, came down with pneumonia. Amazingly, neither Willow nor my Chihuahua fell ill. We assumed it was because they were seniors and had built up a strong immune system.

Ceanna, sadly, did not survive. When we returned home from the emergency hospital after Ceanna's passing, Ellie collapsed in her recliner. Willow jumped up and ran to her to crawl up on her lap and lick away every tear from her face.

At the end of July, I noticed that Willow was having difficulty getting up and down. She was no longer able to climb on the couch. One day, when I returned home from work, she was having trouble remaining on her feet, her gums were white, and her nose was extremely cold, like she had dipped it in a tub of ice water. I rushed her to the vet.

Even after my vet ran tests and put Willow on steroids and antibiotics, she fell ill three more times, and her health went downhill quickly. Then one day Willow could no longer stand or walk, even with assistance, and she stopped eating. We made an appointment at the emergency hospital in Houston where they took X-rays and an ultrasound, which showed tumors on her spleen and other vital organs; she was bleeding internally, too. We had to make the awful and painful decision to let her go.

I don't know why Willow was only with us for such a short time. Maybe it was to comfort us when all the other Collies were sick. Maybe she was here to help me through the death of my mom and grandmother that December. Maybe she was sent to us so that we would do what was right for her when the time came.

All I know is that she was the most devoted, loyal, and loving baby. She blessed my life more than I can ever say.

 *Angela Walker*

Mother's Little Helper

Maya, my small, black-and-white Border Collie-mix, has been my shadow ever since I took her whimpering and trembling from my neighbor's arms. She and her littermates had been abandoned by their owner at an old guard hut on a moshav (communal agricultural village) just outside of Jerusalem, Israel, where I was living. He had taken the pup's mother and disappeared. My neighbor, a young teenage girl, had managed to find homes for all the pups except for Maya, who had a hernia through which her intestines were puffing out, with only a thin layer of skin protecting them. She might have been born with the hernia, or it could've been the result of abuse, but regardless of the cause, nobody wanted a damaged dog. My neighbor was desperate to find Maya a home, as she could not afford a dog needing such medical care.

I was traveling at the time, but the minute I returned home to Jerusalem, my neighbor appeared on my doorstep with Maya in tow. Although I already had three dogs, and my roommate had four street cats, I agreed to take Maya in, thinking I would find her a home once I had her hernia fixed and got her spayed.

Maya had different plans. Within days, she won me over with her gentle eyes and puppy antics. All my other dogs had been rescued as adults, so I was enjoying having a puppy around.

Since then, Maya has always followed me around the house, but her herding tendency only manifested itself once my sons were born. By that time, I had rescued three more dogs and married my husband, who came with a rescued dog of his own.

Because of her gentle and submissive ways, Maya was always on the bottom of the doggie hierarchy along with Jessie, my Poodle/Terrier-mix. But that didn't stop them from standing guard over my first son the day we brought him home from the hospital. As if they had worked out an agreement between themselves, they each took up a position on opposite sides of the crib and did not leave my son's side for three days. The dogs lay alert next to the crib, not allowing anyone near it unless they were accompanied by my husband or me. Even Chico, another Terrier-mix and the alpha dog of the pack, had to creep by on his stomach with his eyes down in order to approach the crib.

When my son started walking, Maya would circle him when we went to the park, and if he wandered off to what she considered to be too far from me, she nervously ran back and forth between us, herding us closer together. At the playground, she trailed my son up the steps and down the slide, weaving in and out of the other children in order to catch up with "her" boy.

When my second son was born, Maya's job became more difficult, as the two boys sometimes walked off in different directions. She was always torn, unsure of which one to stay with. They kept her busy as she ran anxiously between them, circling them and running back to me, tongue hanging out, dancing on her toes as if to say, "What should I do? Who should I follow? Hurry up and go keep them together. What kind of mother are you?"

Today my sweet, beautiful Maya is closing in on 13. She is my constant companion. When I cook, she squeezes between me and the foot of the kitchen counter. When I shower, she opens the bathroom door and curls up next to the tub. When I write, she sleeps inside one of the crates under my desk or at my feet, always with her gentle, black eyes and sharp ears – though her hearing is slowly fading in her old age – alert to my every move.

 Judith Sudilovsky

Night Visitor

Every day an Australian Shepherd/Chow-mix came to visit us. We called her Old Navy because that's where her collar was from. We always walked and played with her before taking her back to her home, which was about a half mile away.

She then started coming in the middle of the night. Around midnight she would find her way through our doggie door, come up two sets of stairs, and jump onto our bed. (Yes, it was pretty weird the first few times we found an extra furry creature in our bed in the middle of the night.) I finally went to the neighbor's house and found out the dog's real name was Emma, and she belonged to their 19-year-old daughter who had moved a number of times, always into places that did not accept dogs.

I mentioned that if they ever needed to put Emma up for adoption, I hoped they would ask me first. Their daughter saw that Emma would be very happy living with us and agreed that we could keep her.

Emma warmed our hearts and our bed for five years before she was diagnosed with cancer. In between some of her chemotherapy sessions, I ran into the young gal who previously owned Emma. She said she was so happy that we had adopted Emma because she would have never been able to give her the medical attention she needed: That made us all feel better.

Emma was the best friend that I will never forget. She camped, hiked, and fished with us. She has been on top of more fourteeners (mountains that are 14,000+ feet high) than most humans who live here in Colorado. We only had six years with Emma, but they were the best years of our lives.

 Sandra Maday

Beanie Baby

Pinto Bean *hated* men when we got her. She came to us after surviving a car wreck. The local vet had been called to the scene and had taken Pinto to her clinic. Pinto needed to have her toe removed, but the owner was unable to give consent. The great folks at the clinic went out on a limb, fixing Pinto up and nursing her back to health. When she was well enough, they contacted New Hope Cattle Dog Rescue & Rehoming for help. We had just lost our Shepherd/ Retriever mix and were happy to take in a foster, as both we and our little dog, Jack, were sad.

Pinto and Jack instantly became two peas in a pod, but with humans Pinto had her issues. She unfortunately had a "man problem," so my husband was a problem for her.

During Pinto's first training session, we had to stop because she was so agitated that we thought her chest was going to explode. Gradually we had a neighbor's son come over and throw treats at her until she figured out that boys were good. Then, when one of our guy friends would come over, we would leave a bowl of small treats on the porch. They would do the same thing: just peg her with treats until she figured it out that they were good. Now, if you watch her with men, you would never believe that she was once scared of them. My husband cradles her like a little baby, and she just melts. When he travels, I get the famous stink-eye from Pinto because she misses her daddy.

Pinto Bean was our first ball nut. Her obsession was absolutely nonstop. Oh, you are going to the bathroom at 3:00 A.M.? Why don't I drop this ball by your feet so you can throw it? Are you taking a shower? Here, I'll put my ball in it for you to make it easier. Great! You're in the yard! Here, let me give you my ball. What? You don't see it? Let me drop it closer. Still don't see it? Hey. Hey! I'm tapping your calf... Throw my ball!

The ball badgering never ended. If her calf-tap didn't work, she'd start barking. She'd stare. She wouldn't accept the throwing of a different ball. It had to be the one she picked out in the morning as her toy for the day. Her love for fetch turned out to be a blessing in disguise because the ball turned out to be as good as a treat to get her to see the value of having men around.

Our little, alpha Beanie baby is a handful, but we consider ourselves lucky to have her. She is a snuggle-bug, an explorer, a fetcher, and an absolute nutbag. She is Pinto, often in her own little world, and we are happy she shares a piece of it with us.

 *Paula Wilderman*

Long Tails Short

Jetstreams and Daydreams: When I received a call from Central Ohio Sheltie Rescue that they had a Blue Heeler/Sheltie-mix for me to foster, I did not hesitate. I met the transport volunteer, received an adorable blue dog called Vincent, and put him in my car. I knew Vincent was special when I saw him watching the airstreams that planes left behind. Vincent knew things about which the other Shelties in my life had no clue. Shelties do not hunt as a general rule; Vincent has an excellent nose for hunting. We have put that nose to work on many occasions to track lost dogs. Vincent is also in charge of chasing the hawk away from our yard. He's a natural when it comes to visiting nursing homes. Watching him work is always a pleasure. When I put his backpack on him, he knows it's time to work. *-Renee Engelbach*

Shadow's Light: Shadow has been quite a character from the beginning. His slight underbite and semi-curled, floppy ears give him a loveable, clownish face. When he came to "try out" for our family, my other dogs took right to him, although one thought it was strange that he didn't have a long tail. She stared at his butt and got the most puzzled look on her face, tilting her head and wrinkling her forehead. Last year Shadow was diagnosed with diabetes. He is on insulin now and has gone blind. Even so, he still comes to the top of the stairs to greet us every time we come home, with his little nub wagging as fast as it did the first day he came to visit. Before adopting Shadow, I had heard that Cattle Dogs were quite the talkers, but I never believed it. Shadow showed me it's true; his bark sounds like he is saying, "I love you." We love you, too, Shadow, and thank you for all the joy you have given us all these years. *-Lisa Ferrell*

Christmas Cookie

J ust before Christmas, my husband and I went into a friend's shop to do some holiday shopping for our two Border Collies, Tiara and Lady. We were getting ready to check out when we saw that she had a picture of a Border Collie she was getting ready to post on Petfinder.com for Gloucester/Mathews Humane Society.

My husband asked, "Is that a Border Collie? A girl? How old?"

We were *not* looking to expand our family, but we went to see Cookie anyway. She was a frightened girl who wanted nothing to do with us. She was so scared that she even charged at me! I did not want to take on the challenge of this dog, but my husband made me feel bad by saying that no one else would adopt her, so we gave her a try.

My first thought after getting her home was, "What have we done?"

Cookie was not an easy girl. She was scared of everything and not affectionate at all. Nevertheless, with the adoption papers signed, we decided to do all we could for her.

A couple of days after adopting Cookie, I came home to check my mail, and there was an envelope containing a tapestry Christmas stocking. I called the company and told them they duplicated the order we'd made two months ago for Lady. It was Lady's first Christmas with us, as we had adopted her in June, also from Gloucester. The company had no record of the shipment.

The mystery Christmas stocking made me think that perhaps Cookie was touched by Christmas Angels and meant to have a stocking on our hearth for years to come. That year hers hung alongside the rest of our packs, which, in retrospect, is a metaphor for how she came to fit in. My Christmas Cookie has become my soul dog; I can't imagine not having her grumpy soul around. I love her more than I could ever explain.

Cookie and I competed for several years in agility together, she achieved her Master Agility titles, and then one day she let me know that she just could not do it any longer. I sure cried that day, but she has also let me know she is enjoying her retirement! Cookie turned a minimum of nine years old that year and must have talked to the Christmas Agility Angels for me, as soon thereafter I found Bryant online at Heritage Humane in Williamsburg. He had been there for over a month and was heartworm positive. We fostered him through Atlantic Region Central Border Collie Rescue, and on December 23rd we officially added him to our family.

Bryant, now known as Dash, was also a bit difficult at first, and he gave us an added challenge by having seizures two weeks into our relationship. Cookie reminded me that we could do this! We treated the heartworms, found ways to manage his seizures, and earned his trust. Dash has turned out to be the best boy for our family: sweet, loyal, and hardworking. He has already achieved several agility titles, and we are becoming an awesome agility team.

The moral of this story is that if you open your heart, listen carefully, and believe in the furry friends who cross your path, perhaps you'll find a special delivery from Christmas Angels for you, too!

 Janice Bryant

Long Road Home

This story begins with a young Hattie serving her military duty down in Georgia. One day she walked by a pet store and spotted a tiny Australian Cattle Dog (ACD) puppy for sale. Hattie couldn't leave the puppy there, and even though she couldn't keep it with her in the barracks, she bought the dog, whom she named Misty, and found someone to care for her until Hattie could take her home to Oregon.

Hattie married, and for seven years Misty had a home, a loving family, and two little boys to supervise. But big changes came one January. Hattie became pregnant again, and the family moved to a brand new home in a new town. Misty, who had developed progressive retinal atrophy (PRA), a genetic condition in ACDs that eventually causes blindness, discovered an escape hole in the new yard. Hattie searched for Misty for several months but never found her. The family was devastated, but they never gave up hope, and Hattie never quit looking for Misty.

That April I received an email from the rescue coordinator at Heartland Humane Society in Corvallis, Oregon. They'd picked up a sweet female Cattle Dog wandering along Highway 34, east of Corvallis. Because she was older and sight-impaired, Heartland knew she'd be hard to place, so they were looking for a rescue to help. Diane, a foster parent in Klamath Falls, said she could take her, so the shelter released Iris to Pet Adoption Network, and Iris made the three-hour trip over Willamette Pass to her foster home.

Iris settled in with Diane and her two dogs, a younger ACD and a senior Jack Russell Terrier. Even though she was losing her sight, Iris enjoyed going out to help "herd" the horses, who were very tolerant of the serious little dog's attempts to keep them in line. She learned "up" and "down" cues for ditch banks, stairs, and hillsides. Her vision continued to deteriorate, but she was happy. When being with the horses became too dangerous due to her vision loss, she was allowed to "work" the pygmy goats instead. They were about Iris' size and didn't mind her attempts to herd them.

For a year and a half, Iris' photo remained on the rescue website, but nobody inquired. Old, blind dogs are just not something most people want to take on. Diane figured Iris was there for the long run, as did the rest of us.

Then a query from Hattie came in: *"I am wondering if it is possible to see a few different pictures besides the ones available on the site. The reason I ask is I lost my Blue Heeler more than a year ago. I searched and searched for her, as I had her since she was a pup. A couple of months after I lost her, I thought I saw her on a newscast about our local Eugene Humane Society. I sent my husband to look for her, but apparently they had adopted her out already.*

Anyway, I always hold out hope that I may find her. This Iris looks almost identical to my lost pet."

The following Saturday Hattie and her family drove to Klamath Falls to meet Iris. In her foster mom's opinion, she displayed behaviors that she'd never exhibited with strangers including being very generous with kisses for Hattie. Hattie and her family decided Iris was indeed their missing girl who had wandered off almost a year and a half before.

We went through our usual adoption process – the application and home visit – because no matter how certain these folks were that this was their "Mimi," we wanted to be sure she was going to a safe, loving home. We appreciated that Hattie was fine with the process; she understood that we cared enough to ensure Iris' well-being. Of course, the family came through with flying colors.

Toward the end of that month, I picked up Iris in Klamath Falls for her return trip over Willamette Pass. It was a tense trip for me; I always feel like I'm carrying a precious cargo when I'm transporting rescued animals, and this little, sight-impaired Cattle Dog hopped into my car with such trust and confidence that the weight of her safety rested extra heavy on my shoulders, especially since an early storm had left the pass slick and slushy with half a foot of new snow not yet plowed. It was a very slow trip; the usually three-hour drive took more like four and a half hours.

When we reached Eugene, Hattie and the children were waiting. Iris didn't flick an eyelash when I lifted her out of the car and Hattie took the leash; she said hello, checked around for treats, and settled into the back of Hattie's van. She seemed to be saying, "Well, that was a nice interlude, and I enjoyed myself, but what took you so long to find me?"

I admit to a few sniffles as I waved goodbye.

The next day I received a note from Hattie: *"Misty has come home. She has already found her walking path in the house and yard. She woke around 2:00 A.M. last night to go to the bathroom and then spent an hour playing. I really enjoyed this. Everyone was asleep but us, and we really got to spend some good quality time together. She is already at ease and seems like the same old Misty. She and my oldest son, Jacob, who spent the most time with her, are back to being best friends already. He spent hours yesterday brushing her and actually cleaned his room, so she could sleep in it. It is so special to see the bond. She also is doing her usual ignoring of the baby, which she always did until they were big enough to give her something. However, the baby sat down this morning with a spoon full of yogurt right in front of her as she was lying down. She gave Misty a bite, and all of a sudden, Misty realized, 'Hey, maybe this baby isn't so bad.' So she took a lick, and then the baby took a lick.*

When Derek came home last night, it was awesome; Misty was resting on Jacob's bed, and he walked in and sat down next to her. She sat up wagging her tale and started licking his arms like she always did.

Anyhow, we are all just so happy, and I once again wanted to thank you."

Helping reunite Misty and her family made that white-knuckle drive over the snow-covered Willamette Pass well worth the new gray hairs. It reminded me again of the many ways that rescues can help bring dogs home.

 Linda Watkins

The Only Counting is on You

Wes after 1 month

Wes after 6 months

I had begun keeping a secret tally: how many foster dogs would I need to save to make up for the one I hadn't been able to? The next dog had to have a success story, and the directors of the foster group agreed that I could use a lesser challenge this time. I needed a dog I could easily train and quickly adopt out. Instead, I got Wes.

He came to my Maryland home from a shelter in Virginia in a crate, curled up in the corner, afraid to come out. He was not one of the beautiful Border Collies whose Internet photos I had pined over, but a skinny thing with a haphazardly cut, dull black coat. His eyes were dilated, which made him seem not just shy but unresponsive. I pleaded for him to come toward me, but there was no response. I reached into his cage, lifted him out, and carried him into the house. I put a collar on him, with an old tag I used for all my fosters. It had only my phone number on it because every dog who had ever worn it belonged to someone else.

Within a few days I was finally able to coax Wes into following me a few feet at a time – not walking but crawling on his stomach. It would take 15 minutes to travel from the bedroom to the kitchen. I'd repeat, "Come, come, Wes. You're safe." To lead him outside, I'd get down on my hands and knees and crawl beside him. On the fifth day, when he stood up and took a few shaky steps, I was exhilarated. This was the feeling I loved: watching a dog begin to grow and trust. But then Wes lifted his leg to urinate on my bed, and then again in the kitchen, and then on my leg. He urinated every few steps, as though it might help him find his way back. He was protecting himself from a danger I knew wasn't there.

Then the vet confirmed my suspicion: Wes was blind. My heart sank because a blind dog would be hard to rehome. I took him away from the vet's office, feeling like we were escaping.

With careful training Wes stopped intentionally marking his way around the house, but he still accidentally urinated while sleeping and walking. It was indeed a medical issue, not a behavioral one. The vet thought it would be curable, but the medications failed one after the other, trapping us in a pattern of waiting, hoping, and restarting. And each time the medication didn't work, we carried the weight of the consequences.

So I began to keep another tally, this time of things that made Wes unadoptable. No one would want a dog who was blind, timid, no longer a puppy. They wouldn't want one who never barked, who urinated often and unpredictably, and who hid more often than he played. People wanted a dog who moved confidently, not one who hugged walls and slinked around furniture to find his way. Not even our other dogs wanted Wes. He was trying to disappear, and they were letting him.

I stopped keeping count when the vet determined Wes's incontinence was, in fact, not curable, that he'd need two doses of medication a day for the rest of his life. Understanding the situation, the vet offered to keep Wes at the clinic and put him to sleep. This was the second time I'd heard this offer, and perhaps for my own protection as much as his, I packed Wes in the car and drove back home, defeated.

I wrote a letter to the directors of the rescue group. Wes is a good dog – a smart dog – but his health wasn't going to get better. I put Wes's future back in their hands and reminded myself, "Wes is *not* mine."

The directors wrote back with the answer I'd feared: I had done all I could – more than they'd asked – and they would come take him away. I pictured Wes in his crate, curled up again, afraid and lonely like he'd been the day I met him. I also knew what inevitably happened to dogs whom no one wanted, but that's a reality that fosters face – should know how to face – so feeling out of options, I agreed to give Wes back. And again, we waited.

Foster dogs aren't your own. They come into your life just long enough to be housetrained, to learn to walk on a leash, to build trust with humans. You determine what kind of household they need – big yards, other dogs, elderly couples, children – and when you find that perfect match, the dogs move to their forever homes. Success is saying goodbye. And if you don't love them too much, it doesn't hurt to let them go.

Celebration has a way of sneaking up on grief, so when my son, Cameron, adopted a puppy from our local shelter, it felt good to rejoice. Cameron was a new graduate, about to start an exciting stage of his life in a new place: He needed a young, healthy dog who could keep up with him, and they were a happy match from the start. But when Cameron brought me with him on an errand to the pet store, I couldn't stop thinking of Wes at home, no longer huddled in a corner, but instead comfortably basking in a square of sunlight. With a past full of humans who had neglected, abused, and betrayed him, Wes had decided to trust me. This quality in dogs, the ability to replace distrust with total faith, is one of the most special things I've ever witnessed. Wes could show someone else that inspiring, unselfish trust, but because of some biological bad luck, he'd never get the chance.

On our way out of the store, Cameron stopped to make his puppy a nametag. And then, almost without knowing what my hands were doing, I ordered a nametag, too. I typed my phone number and above that the name Wes. When I left the store with the tag, I had the revelation that I was bringing it home not just to *a* dog, but to *my* dog.

In one of those moments where you silence all the no's in your mind and listen for that one faint yes, I wrote a letter to the foster director. "Don't come," I said. "I'm keeping him."

Wes must have needed to hear someone say yes because since then, his damaged spirit has healed. His coat has grown back lustrous and full. When I walk him on a leash, which he trusts me to do, people compliment him. No one would guess he's blind by the way he holds his head up, proud. Wes plays outside, greets visitors, and wags his tail with abandon. He has become the happy dog I thought I needed to foster. I'd tried so hard to get him ready to be someone else's that I hadn't noticed he was becoming mine. And now all those tally marks don't matter – just the ten digits on his tag that tell the world I'm his, too.

 Carolyn Sabol and Hayley Huntley

About Happy Tails Books™

Schnauzer Chihuahua Golden Retriever PUG

DACHSHUND German Shepherd Collie Boxer

Labrador Retriever Husky Beagle ALL AMERICAN

Border Collie Pit Bull Terrier Shih Tzu Miniature Pinscher

Chow Chow Australian Shepherd Rottweiler Greyhound

Boston Terrier Jack Russell Poodle Cocker Spaniel

GREAT DANE Doberman Pinscher Yorkie SHEEPDOG

ST. BERNARD Pointer Blue Heeler

Happy Tails Books™ was created to support animal rescue efforts by showcasing the love and joy adopted dogs have to offer. With the help of animal rescue groups, stories are submitted by people who have adopted dogs, and then Happy Tails Books™ compiles them into breed-specific books. These books serve not only to entertain but also to educate readers about dog adoption and the characteristics of each specific type of dog. Happy Tails Books™ donates a significant portion of proceeds back to the rescue groups that help gather stories for the books.

Happy Tails Books™

To submit a story or learn about other books Happy Tails Books™ publishes, please visit our website at http://happytailsbooks.com.

Ava DuVernay

Movie Director

by Kate Moening

BLASTOFF! READERS

2

BELLWETHER MEDIA • MINNEAPOLIS, MN

Blastoff! Readers are carefully developed by literacy experts to build reading stamina and move students toward fluency by combining standards-based content with developmentally appropriate text.

LEVELS

Level 1 provides the most support through repetition of high-frequency words, light text, predictable sentence patterns, and strong visual support.

Level 2 offers early readers a bit more challenge through varied sentences, increased text load, and text-supportive special features.

Level 3 advances early-fluent readers toward fluency through increased text load, less reliance on photos, advancing concepts, longer sentences, and more complex special features.

★ **Blastoff! Universe**

Reading Level

BLASTOFF! Beginners
Grade **K**

BLASTOFF! READERS
Grades **1–3**

BLASTOFF! DISCOVERY
Grade **4**

This edition first published in 2021 by Bellwether Media, Inc.

No part of this publication may be reproduced in whole or in part without written permission of the publisher. For information regarding permission, write to Bellwether Media, Inc., Attention: Permissions Department, 6012 Blue Circle Drive, Minnetonka, MN 55343.

Library of Congress Cataloging-in-Publication Data
Names: Moening, Kate, author.
Title: Ava DuVernay : movie director / Kate Moening.
Description: Minneapolis, MN : Bellwether Media, 2021. | Series: Blastoff! readers: women leading the way | Includes bibliographical references and index. | Audience: Ages 5-8 | Audience: Grades K-1 | Summary: "Relevant images match informative text in this introduction to Ava DuVernay. Intended for students in kindergarten through third grade"– Provided by publisher.
Identifiers: LCCN 2019053860 (print) | LCCN 2019053861 (ebook) | ISBN 9781644872079 (library binding) | ISBN 9781681038315 (paperback) | ISBN 9781618919656 (ebook)
Subjects: LCSH: Duvernay, Ava-Juvenile literature. | Motion picture producers and directors–United States–Biography. | African American motion picture producers and directors–Biography. | Women motion picture producers and directors–United States–Biography.
Classification: LCC PN1998.3.D9255 M64 2021 (print) | LCC PN1998.3.D9255 (ebook) | DDC 791.4302/33092 [B]–dc23
LC record available at https://lccn.loc.gov/2019053860
LC ebook record available at https://lccn.loc.gov/2019053861

Editor: Elizabeth Neuenfeldt   Designer: Andrea Schneider

Printed in the United States of America, North Mankato, MN.